BUSINESS
Challenges

LONGMAN Challenges

COURSE BOOK

nina o'driscoll

fiona scott-barrett

Longman Business English

Map of the Book

	UNIT	PAGE	TOPICS	LANGUAGE	VOCABULARY AREAS	OTHER LEARNING POINTS
9	Career Development	32	Asking for and giving information about career development	Simple past: verb **be – was/were** Simple past: regular verbs Prepositions: **from...to, in, for**	Career development	**Numberwork:** Years
10	Company History	35	Asking for and giving information about company history	Simple past: irregular verbs Time expression: **ago**	Company history	**Tactics:** Asking for information again Checking you have the right information
11	Past Performance	38	Describing trends	Simple past Adverbs: **slightly, steadily, sharply** Prepositions: **from, to, by**	Trends	Describing a graph **Skills:** Reading (car sales)
12	Small Talk	41	Making conversation with people you know	Greeting people you know	Adjectives	**Conversation:** Asking general and specific questions **Wordwork:** Adjectives and modifiers – **good/very good/not very good** etc. **Culture:** Topics of conversation
13	Directions	44	Asking and explaining how to get to places	Asking for and giving directions Explaining location Imperatives: **take..., don't go...** Prepositions of location	Directions Landmarks	**Numberwork:** Ordinal numbers – **1st, 2nd** etc. **Learning Tip:** Organising and recording vocabulary
14	Guidelines	47	Explaining guidelines	Modal verbs: **must, mustn't, should, don't have to** Make sure you..., avoid...	Travel	**Skills:** Reading (jet lag) Listening (business in India)
15	Telephone Calls	50	Exchanging information on the telephone	Answering the telephone Getting through	Telephoning	Spelling **Culture:** The start of a call **Tactics:** Controlling the conversation
16	Offers and Requests	53	Asking for and offering help Leaving and taking telephone messages	Making offers: **Would you like to...?, I'll...** Making requests: **Could you...?** Pronouns: **me/you/him** etc.		**Numberwork:** Telephone numbers **Conversation:** Sounding polite
	Project Unit: A Top Firm	56				

UNIT	PAGE	TOPICS	LANGUAGE	VOCABULARY AREAS	OTHER LEARNING POINTS
17 Plans	58	Asking for and giving information about plans	Present continuous with future meaning Preposition: **until**	Time expressions	**Learning Tip:** Accuracy v fluency
18 Appointments	61	Arranging appointments	Suggesting dates and times Agreeing to dates and times	Dates and times	**Tactics:** Confirming dates and times **Numberwork:** Dates
19 Products	64	Describing the function and features of a product	It's for... Is/Are designed for... Is/Are available in... Modal verb: **can**	Product description	**Numberwork:** Dimensions **Wordwork:** Word-building – quick/quickly etc. **Skills:** Listening (coffee machines) Writing (a letter)
20 Invitations	67	Making and replying to invitations	Inviting Accepting Declining	Likes and dislikes	**Conversation:** Making successful invitations
21 Comparing Products and Services	70	Comparing products and services	Comparatives and superlatives: **faster/the fastest, more expensive/the most expensive, less time/the least time** etc.	Service description	
22 Working Practices	73	Comparing working practices in different countries	Making comparisons: **not as long as** Showing similarity: **the same**	Working practices	**Numberwork:** Symbols, percentages **Wordwork:** Word-building – **difference/different** etc. **Skills:** Listening (the Netherlands) Reading (Ireland and Greece)
23 Discussions	76	Discussing suggestions about company problems	Asking what people think Agreeing and disagreeing	Workplace trends	**Tactics:** Summarising
24 Restaurants	79	Asking for and giving help with a menu	**What do you recommend?** **Why don't you try...?** **I'll have the...**	Food Methods of cooking	**Tactics:** Explaining dishes **Learning Tip:** Pronunciation
Project Unit: A New Office	82				

Jobs and Professions

A At a medical conference

1 Preview

The people in the pictures meet for the first time.

What questions do they ask?

2 Language Focus

2.1 📻 **Listen to two conversations. Match the conversations and the pictures.**

Conversation 1 Picture ☐
Conversation 2 Picture ☐

2.2 What are the missing words?

Conversation 1

BOB   .... on holiday?

ANNE No, ... on business.

BOB   Oh, really. What ..... you ..... ?

ANNE ..... an accountant.
          I ..... for Total in Jakarta.

Conversation 2

PAUL   ..... you work here in Glasgow?

JOHN   No, ... I ..... in a hospital in Edinburgh.

PAUL   Oh, do you? Do ..... know Dr Stevens?

JOHN   Carl Stevens. Yes, ... He's my boss.

2.3 📻 **Listen again. Are your words the same as the words on the cassette?**

LANGUAGE SUMMARY

Yes/No questions: verb be

QUESTIONS		ANSWERS
Are you	on holiday?	Yes, I **am**.
	on business?	No, I'**m** not.
		No, I'**m** on business. / on holiday.

Yes/No questions: simple present

QUESTIONS		ANSWERS
Do you	**know** Dr Stevens?	Yes, I **do**.
	work in Glasgow?	No, I **don't**.
		No, I **work** in Edinburgh.

Open questions: simple present

QUESTIONS	ANSWERS
What **do** you **do**?	I'**m** an accountant.
	I **work** for Total in Jakarta.
	I **work** in a hospital.

Prepositions
for Total   **in** Jakarta   **in** a hospital

CHECK!

1 With the simple present, you use do in

	Yes	No
a) questions.	☐	☐
b) long answers.	☐	☐
c) short answers.	☐	☐

2 Put do in these sentences.
   a) you work in Jakarta?   b) Yes, I.   c) What you do?

B On a plane to Singapore and Jakarta

3 Speechwork

3.1 📼 **Listen and underline the stressed words.**

Example: Do you <u>work</u> in <u>Bonn</u>?

1 Do you work in Bonn?
2 What do you do?
3 Do you know Tom?
4 Do you live in Rome?

3.2 📼 **Listen to two sounds. Do you hear sound 1 or sound 2 in these sentences?**

	1	2
1 Do you work in Rome?	☐	☐
2 Yes, I do.	☐	☐
3 Do you live there too?	☐	☐

4 Wordwork

4.1 Look at the identity cards. Complete them with words from the lists.

Jobs	Activities
accountant	buy ✓
administrator ✓	do
engineer	give
tax expert	manage
sales representative	sell

KEATINGS

NAME: Helen Brown
JOB: Buyer
ACTIVITY: I .buy. food products.

Examples

CFi

NAME: Marie Duval
JOB: Administrator
ACTIVITY: I organise training courses.

P B X

1 NAME: Eva Engstrom
JOB: .....
ACTIVITY: I .....computer systems.

Wilcox International

2 NAME: Alec Macfarlane
JOB: .....
ACTIVITY: I .....building projects.

3 **P B X**

NAME: Pat March
JOB: .....
ACTIVITY: I .....the company accounts.

Park & Moss

4 NAME: Christine Saville
JOB: .....
ACTIVITY: I .....tax advice.

4.2 📟 **Listen. Are your words the same as the words on the cassette?**

4.3 📟 **Listen. How many syllables do you hear?**

Example: accountant = ac/coun/tant = 3

1 accountant
2 administrator
3 buyer
4 engineer
5 expert
6 representative

4.4 📟 **Listen again. Underline the stressed syllables.**

Example: ac<u>coun</u>tant

> **CHECK!**
>
> **1 When do you use an?**
> I'm an accountant.   I'm an engineer.
> I'm a buyer.   I'm a tax expert.
> **2 Put a or an in these sentences.**
>   a) I'm . . . . . administrator.
>   b) I'm . . . . . sales representative.

4.5 Complete these sentences about you.

1 I work for . . . . . .
2 I'm a/an . . . . . .
3 I . . . . . .

4.6 Work with a partner and have a conversation.

Model
A What's your name?
B I'm . . . . . .
A And what do you do?
B I'm a/an . . . . . . I . . . . . .

5 Practice

> **CHECK!**
>
> **When do you use for and when do you use in?**
> I work for CFI.   I work in a training centre.
> I live in Paris.

5.1 Read about four people and their jobs. What are the missing words – for or in?

1 I'm a personal assistant. I work . . . . . Honda, a car company. I don't type letters; I organise travel for my boss and deal with visitors. I live and work . . . . . Swindon.
2 I work . . . . . Honda. I'm a sales representative. I'm . . . . . Swindon on business but I don't live here. I live . . . . . Tokyo.
3 I'm an engineer. I design car engines. I work . . . . . Honda . . . . . the Swindon car plant. I also live . . . . . Swindon.
4 I'm . . . . . Swindon on holiday. My parents live here. I'm an accountant. I work . . . . . Arthur Andersen . . . . . Tokyo.

5.2 Work in groups. Choose one of the people in 5.1. Other students ask you questions and try to guess who you are.

6 Output

6.1 What do you do? Make notes about your job.

Company or organisation
Job
Activity
Town or city

6.2 Work with a partner and have a conversation.

Roles	You are yourselves.
Relationship	You don't know each other.
Place	On a plane.
Topics	Your jobs and organisations.

Business Contacts

1 Preview

Your boss organises a business meeting for you. You want information about the people at the meeting.

1.1 What information do you want? Choose four points from the list.

jobs   positions   companies   ages
activities   interests   places of work

1.2 What do you say to get the information?

2 Language Focus

2.1 Look at the memo. What is it about?

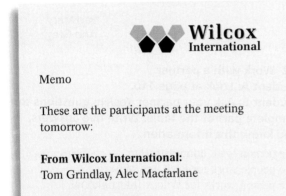

Wilcox International

Memo

These are the participants at the meeting tomorrow:

From Wilcox International:
Tom Grindlay, Alec Macfarlane

From Park and Moss:
Peter Martin, Christine Saville, Karen Page, Wolfgang Binder

2.2 Look at the business cards. Complete these sentences.

1 Wilcox International is a . . . . . company.
2 Park and Moss are . . . .

Alec Macfarlane is a new employee of Wilcox International. Tom Grindlay tells him about the participants at tomorrow's meeting.

2.3 🔲 Listen and complete the table.

	Job	Place of work
1 Peter		
2 Christine		
3 Karen		
4 Wolfgang		

2.4 Match words from A and B to make complete sentences.

Example: 1 = b

A	B
1 Is he a	a) for Park and Moss?
2 He works in	b) director of Park and Moss?
3 What does	c) they work?
4 Karen Page is	d) boss.
5 Where do	e) their London office.
6 Does he work	f) her assistant.
7 He's Klaus Daniel's	g) she do?

2.5 🔲 Listen again. Are your sentences the same as the sentences on the cassette?

Tom Grindlay
MANAGING DIRECTOR

Wilcox International

CONSTRUCTION

Park & Moss
Germany

Accountants

Wolfgang Binder
Manager

LANGUAGE SUMMARY

Yes/No questions: verb be

QUESTIONS	ANSWERS
	Yes, he **is**.
Is he a director?	No, he **isn't**.
	No, he**'s** the Sales Manager.

Yes/No questions: simple present

QUESTIONS	ANSWERS
	Yes, he **does**.
Does he **work** for Park and Moss?	No, he **doesn't**.
	No, he **works** for PBX.

Open questions: simple present

QUESTIONS	ANSWERS
What **does** she **do**?	She **works** for Park and Moss.
	She**'s** their tax expert.
Where	**do** they / **does** he **work**?	In their London office.

Possessives
She's **my/your/his/her/our/their** assistant.
Wolfgang Binder is Klaus Daniel**'s** boss.

CHECK!

1 When do you use **does** in questions?
2 When do you add **s** to a verb?
3 Make sentences.
   a) Where/she/live?
   b) She/live/in Spain.
   c) What/she/do?

---

3 Speechwork

📃 **When you add s to a verb you can make three sounds. Listen. Do you hear sound 1, sound 2 or sound 3?**

	1	2	3
1 organises	☐	☐	☑
2 buys	☐	☐	☐
3 does	☐	☐	☐
4 gives	☐	☐	☐
5 manages	☐	☐	☐
6 types	☐	☐	☐

4 Practice

You work for Colours International, a paint manufacturer.

4.1 Look at the organigram. Tell a visitor about your company.

Models
Peter Black is our Managing Director.
David Tan is his Personal Assistant.

COLOURS INTERNATIONAL

Managing Director Peter Black
Personal Assistant David Tan
Sales Manager John White
Personnel Manager Jane Brown
Assistant **You!**
Assistant Mary Green
Secretary Ann Grey

4.2 Work with a partner.
Student A: Look at page 110.
Student B: Ask your partner Yes/No questions to complete part of the table. Write five answers. You know this information.

one person is an administrator
two people work for Park and Moss
one person works for Wilcox International
one person works in London

	Company	Job	City
Yoshi			
Tony			
Kate			

Now ask questions with what and where. Complete the rest of the table.

4.3 Now answer your partner's questions about these people.

	Company	Job	City
Mary-Jo	Keatings	Buyer	Dublin
Pablo	PBX	Sales Representative	Madrid
Tim	PBX	Engineer	Hong Kong

5 Wordwork

5.1 Match the words and logos.

Example: 1 = D

1 construction
2 fashion
3 furniture
4 oil
5 publishing
6 travel

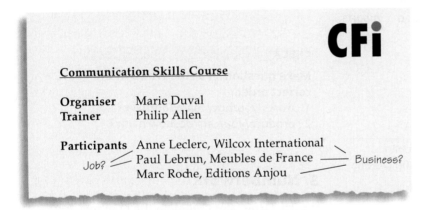

5.2 Make sentences like this. Use the information in 5.1.

Example: Taylor Woodrow are in the construction business.

6 Tactics Focus

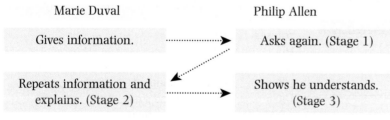

Communication Skills Course

Organiser Marie Duval
Trainer Philip Allen

Participants Anne Leclerc, Wilcox International
Job? Paul Lebrun, Meubles de France — *Business?*
Marc Roche, Editions Anjou

Marie Duval of CFI tells Philip Allen about the course participants.

6.1 🖭 Listen to their telephone conversation. What are the participants' jobs and businesses?

6.2 Look at this conversation plan.

Marie Duval		Philip Allen
Gives information.	·····>	Asks again. (Stage 1)
Repeats information and explains. (Stage 2)	·····>	Shows he understands. (Stage 3)

Read these sentences and match them with the stages on the conversation plan.

1 Wilcox International. They're in the construction business.
2 Sorry, who does she work for?
3 Right.
4 Sorry, what does he do?
5 I see.
6 He's a designer. He designs furniture.

6.3 🖭 Now listen to their conversation again and check your answers.

TACTICS SUMMARY

When you don't hear or you don't understand information, ask again.
Sorry, who does he work for?
Sorry, what does he do?

When somebody stops you, repeat information and explain it.
Wilcox International. They're in the construction business.
He's a designer. He designs furniture.

When you understand, show it.
Right.
I see.

7 Practice

Work with a partner and have conversations about people you know.

Model
A My friend/sister/brother works for ....
B Sorry, who does he/she work for?
A .... They're in the ..... business.
B I see. And what does he/she do?
A He/she's a/an ....
B Sorry, what does he/she do?
A He/she's a/an ....
He/she ....

8 Output

8.1 Think of a famous person. Make notes about him or her.

8.2 Work in groups. Other students try to guess who your famous person is. Take turns to ask and answer questions.

3

Company Information

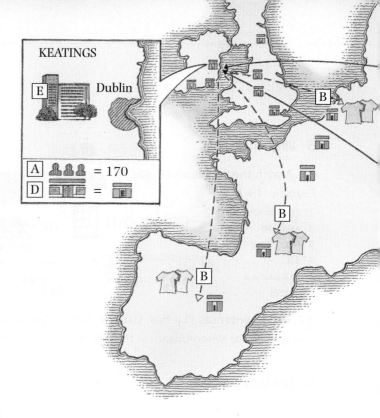

KEATINGS

E　Dublin

A 　= 170
D 　=

1 Preview

Keatings is an international chain of stores based in Ireland. They sell food and clothes. They buy food products from Palumbo in Italy.

Match the letters on the map with words from this list.

Example: D = stores

employees (x 2)　Head Office (x 2)　products
exports　stores　factory (x 2)　production　imports

2 Language Focus

Match the questions and answers.

Example: 1 = d

Questions	Answers
1 Where are Keatings' main markets?	a) In Dublin.
2 What does Palumbo produce?	b) 20,000 per day.
3 Where is Keatings based?	c) 170.
4 How many employees do they have at their Head Office?	d) Ireland, the UK, France, Spain and Holland.
5 How many factories does Palumbo have?	e) Clothes.
6 How many tins of tomatoes do they produce?	f) Pasta and tinned tomatoes.
7 What does Keatings export?	g) 2.

LANGUAGE SUMMARY

Open questions: verb be
Where **are** Keatings' main markets?
Where **is** Keatings based?

Open questions: simple present
How many employees **do** they **have**?
How many factories **does** Palumbo **have**?
How many tins of tomatoes **do** they **produce**?

CHECK!

Make questions. Put the words in the correct order.
1 stores/you/how many/do/have?
2 produce/you/cars/do/how many?

3 Numberwork

3.1 🔊 **Listen and underline the numbers you hear.**

Example: 13 or 30

1　13 or 30	4　20,000 or 200,000
2　18 or 80	5　45,000 or 450,000
3　170 or 1,700	6　40,000 or 4,000,000

NUMBERWORK SUMMARY

You see	You say
16	sixteen
60	sixty
100	a (or one) hundred
160	a hundred and sixty
1,000	a (or one) thousand
1,600	one thousand six hundred
16,000	sixteen thousand
16,600	sixteen thousand six hundred
60,000	sixty thousand
600,000	six hundred thousand
660,000	six hundred and sixty thousand
6,000,000	six million

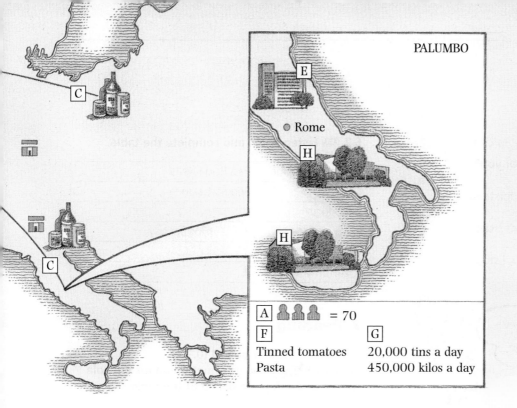

Rome

A	👥👥👥 = 70
F		G
Tinned tomatoes		20,000 tins a day
Pasta		450,000 kilos a day

3.2 📼 **Listen to the numbers in the Numberwork Summary. Underline the stressed syllables.**

Examples: six<u>teen</u>   <u>six</u>ty

3.3 Work with a partner.
Student A: Look at page 110.
Student B: Ask and answer questions to complete the table.

Model
B   What do you have in G1?
A   116. What do you have in G2?
B   3,400.

	1	2	3	4
G		3,400		1,100
R		220		90,000
I		3,000,000	160	
D			570	25,000

4 Practice

Work with a partner. Look again at the map. Ask and answer questions with how many. Ask about these points.

stores   employees at Keatings' Head Office   factories
kilos of pasta   tins of tomatoes

5 Wordwork

5.1 Complete the list.

Verbs	Nouns
design	designer
produce	1 . . . . .
2	buyer
manufacture	3 . . . . .
4	supplier
export	5 . . . . .
6	importer

5.2 Complete these sentences. Use the words in the list in 5.1.

Example: Calvin Klein designs clothes. Yves Saint Laurent is another famous designer.

1   Calvin Klein designs clothes. Yves Saint Laurent is another famous . . . . . .
2   Helen Brown buys food products for Keatings. Her assistant, Jonathan Fox, is also a . . . . . .
3   Nissan manufactures cars. Honda is another Japanese car . . . . . .
4   Italy exports olive oil. Greece is also an olive oil . . . . . .
5   Buitoni produce pasta. Another pasta . . . . . is Mennucci.
6   Bosch . . . . . parts to car manufacturers. Unipart is also a car parts supplier.
7   Godwin and Godwin . . . . . wine to the UK. Allied Domecq are also wine importers.

13

Are these sentences true for you?

	Yes	No
1 When I listen, I try to understand every word.	☐	☐
2 When I listen, I try to understand the important words.	☐	☐
3 When I don't understand, I stop listening.	☐	☐

- It isn't necessary to understand every word in a conversation.
- When you don't understand, continue to listen. Often the meaning becomes clear later in the conversation.

6 Listening

Helen Brown, a buyer for Keatings, is visiting Pastificio Rivella, an Italian supplier. She is talking to Maurizio Rivella, the Managing Director.

6.1 ▭ Listen and answer these questions.

1 Is it the start or the end of the meeting?
2 Is it Helen Brown's first visit to Pastificio Rivella?

6.2 ▭ Listen again and complete the table.

Company name	Pastificio Rivella
Based in	Reggio Calabria
Products	1
Production	2 . . . . . kilos per day
Employees	3
Main markets	4

7 Reading

Student A: Look at page 110.
Student B: Read the information about Vinicola Ambra and complete part B of the table.

Vinicola Ambra

The company, based near Rome, is a producer of quality wines. It supplies restaurants and supermarkets in the region. It uses very modern equipment and technology for its wine-making and so has only eighteen employees. The production is 4,000,000 litres per year. Vinicola Ambra exports mainly to Germany and Sweden.

	A Molitano	B Vinicola Ambra
Based in		
Products		
Production	. . . . . bottles per hour	. . . . . litres per year
Employees		
Main markets		

8 Output

8.1 Work with a partner. Ask questions about Molitano and complete part A of the table.

8.2 Now answer your partner's questions about Vinicola Ambra.

4

Visits

1 Preview

A visitor comes to your organisation for a meeting.

What do you do when he/she arrives?

What do you say?

2 Language Focus

The people below work for Keatings.

2.1 Read their descriptions and answer these questions.

1 Who's the Personnel Manager?
2 Who's responsible for quality control?

2.2 What words in the descriptions tell you

1 somebody's position in the company?
2 about somebody's responsibilities?

Who does what at Keatings?

Patrick Mulligan is the Purchasing Manager. He's responsible for buying food products and clothes for the stores. He's also responsible for quality control.

Moira Thomson is the Personnel Manager. She's responsible for recruiting and training staff for the stores.

LANGUAGE SUMMARY		
Questions		
Who's	the Personnel Manager?	
	the head of the Personnel Department?	
	responsible for recruiting staff?	

Position		
She's	the head of the	Personnel Department.
He's		Special Projects Team.
He's	the	Purchasing Manager.
She's		Information Systems Manager.

Responsibilities		
He's	responsible for	quality control.
She's		Keatings' computer systems.
He's	responsible for	buying food products.
She's		recruiting staff.

CHECK!

1 **When you use a verb after responsible for, which form do you use?**
2 **Make sentences.**
   a) She/responsible for/sell/products.
   b) He/responsible for/design/car engines.

3 Practice

Work with a partner. Ask and answer questions about Keatings.

Model
A Who's the head of the Purchasing Department?
B Patrick Mulligan is. Who's responsible for recruiting staff?
A Moira Thomson is.

Brendan Glass is the head of the Special Projects Team. His team is responsible for choosing sites for new stores.

Jane O'Connor is the head of the Information Systems Department. She's responsible for Keatings' computer systems.

4 Wordwork

4.1 Match the departments and responsibilities.

Example: 1 = c

Departments	Responsibilities
1 production	a) selling products
2 finance	b) distributing products
3 publicity	c) manufacturing products
4 research and	d) developing new products
development	e) doing the company accounts
5 sales	f) publicising the company
6 distribution	

4.2 Make sentences like this. Use the information in 4.1.

Example: The Production Department is responsible for manufacturing products.

4.3 Complete these sentences about you.

1 I work in the . . . . . Department./
I'm the head of the . . . . . Department.
2 I'm responsible for . . . . . .

5 Conversation Focus

Paolo Rosso, Molitano's Sales Manager, visits Keatings. Patrick Mulligan meets him at reception. It is their first meeting.

5.1 Read this conversation. The underlined parts are not appropriate for the situation. How can you change them?

PATRICK MULLIGAN	Welcome to Keatings. I'm Patrick Mulligan. <u>Good morning</u>.
PAOLO ROSSO	<u>Good morning</u>, Mr Mulligan.
PATRICK MULLIGAN	The meeting room isn't far from here. Come this way, please. Here we are. Helen Brown will be here soon. <u>Give me your coat</u>.
PAOLO ROSSO	Oh, thank you.
PATRICK MULLIGAN	<u>Do you want</u> a coffee?
PAOLO ROSSO	Yes, please.
PATRICK MULLIGAN	Sharon, can you bring us two coffees, please? Ah, here's Helen. Mr Rosso, this is Helen Brown, one of our buyers. Helen, this is Paolo Rosso from Molitano.
HELEN BROWN	Pleased to meet you, Mr Rosso.
PATRICK MULLIGAN	<u>Oh, hello, Helen</u>.

5.2 📼 Now listen to the real conversation. What do they say?

CONVERSATION SUMMARY

Introducing

This is	Helen Brown, one of our buyers.
	Paolo Rosso from Molitano.

Greeting

A	B
How do you do?	How do you do?
Pleased to meet you.	Pleased to meet you, too.

Helping

Can I	take your coat?	Thank you.
	get you a coffee?	Yes, please.

6 Speechwork

📼 **Listen and underline the stressed syllables.**

Example: <u>Wel</u>come to <u>Kea</u>tings.

1 Welcome to Keatings.
2 How do you do?
3 Pleased to meet you.
4 Pleased to meet you, too.
5 Can I take your coat?
6 Can I get you a coffee?

7 Culture Focus

7.1 Answer these questions about your country.

1 Do you give your business card
  a) before a meeting?
  b) during a meeting?
  c) at the end of a meeting?
2 When you meet people, do you shake hands
  a) every time you meet?
  b) only when you meet for the first time?
3 When you introduce people, do you use their
  a) title, first name and family name?
  b) title and family name?
  c) first name and family name?

7.2 Answer the same questions about another country you know well.

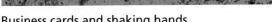

Business cards and shaking hands
Customs are different in different countries. Before you visit a new country, find out what people do.

Names
The use of names and titles is different in different countries. In English-speaking countries you use the first name and family name when you introduce people. When you go to other countries, it is a good idea to follow your host's use of names.

8 Practice

Look at the pictures. What would you say in these situations?

9 Output

9.1 Work in groups of three. Find out about your partners' company names, positions and responsibilities.

9.2 Now have three conversations. Take turns to be A, B and C.

Roles	You are yourselves.
Relationships	A knows B and C. B does not know C. C is a visitor.
Place	In A's office.

Conversation Plan
A Introduce B to C. Explain B's position and responsibilities. Then introduce C to B and give C's company name.
B Greet C.
C Greet B.

Routines

1 Preview

Answer these questions about your routine.

	Yes	No	It depends
1 Do you start work before 8.00 a.m.?	☐	☐	☐
2 Do you drive to work?	☐	☐	☐
3 Do you go home for lunch?	☐	☐	☐
4 Do you go out for business lunches?	☐	☐	☐
5 Do you go out in the evening with clients or colleagues?	☐	☐	☐
6 Do you take work home?	☐	☐	☐

2 Language Focus

PBX is a computer software company. Pat March is an accountant with their UK company in Birmingham.

2.1 Read the interview with Pat from PBX's company magazine.

INTERVIEWER ¹ . . . . .

PAT MARCH Well, I don't live near the office, so I drive to work.

INTERVIEWER ² . . . . .

PAT MARCH About an hour. It depends on the traffic.

INTERVIEWER ³ . . . . .

PAT MARCH I start work at about 8.00 a.m. I'm usually there before my assistant arrives. That gives me time to plan the day.

INTERVIEWER ⁴ . . . . .

PAT MARCH Yes. I usually have a sandwich at my desk. Twice a week I have lunch in the canteen with colleagues, and we sometimes go out for lunch in a pub.

INTERVIEWER ⁵ . . . . .

PAT MARCH I always leave at 4.00 p.m. I have two small children, so I never stay late in the office, but I often take work home to do in the evening. I have a computer at home.

2.2 Complete the interview with these questions.

a) What time do you start work?
b) Do you have lunch at the office?
c) How long does it take?
d) When do you leave work?
e) How do you get to work?

2.3 Read the interview again and complete these sentences.

1 Pat always . . . . . .
2 She's usually . . . . . .
3 She usually . . . . . .
4 She often . . . . . .
5 She sometimes . . . . . .
6 She never . . . . . .
7 Twice a week Pat . . . . . .

LANGUAGE SUMMARY

Questions

When What time	do you	start work? leave work?

How do you get to work?
How long does it take?

Adverbs of frequency

I **always** leave at 4.00 p.m.
I'm **usually** in the office before my assistant arrives.
I **usually** have a sandwich at my desk.
I **often** take work home.
We **sometimes** go out for lunch in a pub.
I **never** stay late in the office.

Expressions of frequency

Once Twice Three times	a week I have lunch in the canteen.

CHECK!

1 **Put these words in the appropriate place on the line.**

always   never   often   sometimes   usually

```
|_____|
0%                                    100%
```

2 **Put never in these sentences.**
a) I get up before 7.00 a.m.
b) He is at home in the evening.

3 Practice

Work with a partner. Ask and answer questions about these points.

1 have lunch in the canteen
2 have meetings in English
3 drive to work
4 go out in the evening with colleagues
5 take work home

Model
A Do you have lunch in the canteen?
B No, I don't. I never have lunch there./Yes. I usually have lunch in the canteen, but I sometimes go out for business lunches.

4 Numberwork

4.1 Match times from A and B with the same meaning.

Example: 1 = b

A		B
1	12.00	a) seven o'clock in the evening
2	7.00 a.m.	b) midday
3	7.00 p.m.	c) half past seven
4	4.00 p.m.	d) seven o'clock in the morning
5	7.15	e) midnight
6	7.30	f) quarter past seven
7	7.45	g) quarter to eight
8	0.00	h) four o'clock in the afternoon

NUMBERWORK SUMMARY

You see	You say
0.00	midnight
6.00 a.m.	six o'clock in the morning *or* six a.m.
6.15	quarter past six *or* six fifteen
6.30	half past six *or* six thirty
6.45	quarter to seven *or* six forty-five
2.00 p.m.	two o'clock in the afternoon *or* two p.m.
6.00 p.m.	six o'clock in the evening *or* six p.m.
12.00	midday *or* noon

4.2 How do you say these times?

1 8.30   3 3.45   5 6.00 a.m.
2 12.30   4 9.15   6 8.00 p.m.

5 Speechwork

5.1 ▭ Listen to four sentences. How many words do you hear in each sentence?

5.2 What sound do you hear in the underlined part of these words?

<u>a</u>t   <u>a</u>bout   <u>o</u>'clock

6 Practice

6.1 Which of these sentences is not a correct answer to the question?

1 How do you get to work?
   a) I walk.
   b) I take the bus.
   c) At 9 o'clock.
   d) I drive.
   e) I take the train.
2 How long does it take?
   a) About half an hour.
   b) I take a long time.
   c) Yes, a long time.
   d) It takes 20 minutes.
3 What time do you get to work?
   a) At about 8.00.
   b) At 8.00.
   c) In the morning.
   d) At 8.00 in the morning.

6.2 Work in groups. Ask and answer questions about the start of other people's working days. Complete the table.

Name	
How?	
How long?	
What time?	

6.3 Read this article from PBX's company magazine. What are the missing words – in or at?

P B X

Takashi Soto is a buyer with PBX in Osaka. He lives in a suburb of Osaka and takes the train to work. It takes forty-five minutes. He usually gets to his office ¹..... 9.00 a.m. ²..... the morning he usually has meetings with suppliers and he sometimes goes out for lunch with them. He usually leaves work ³..... about 6.00 p.m. and three times a week he goes out for dinner and drinks with his colleagues ⁴..... the evening.

Peter Schmidt is an engineer with PBX in Frankfurt. The chart shows his typical week.

6.4 Talk about Peter's routine. Use always, never, sometimes, usually, twice a week or three times a week.

	M	T	W	T	F
leave home 7.00 a.m.	✓	✓	✓	✓	✓
get to work 7.30 a.m.	✓	✓	.	✓	✓
a.m. – meeting with colleagues	✓	.	✓	.	✓
lunch in the canteen	✓	✓	✓	.	✓
p.m. – work alone	✓	✓	✓	✓	✓
leave work 4.00 p.m.	✓	.	.	✓	.
out with colleagues after work	.	.	.	.	.

P B X

Peter Schmidt works in Frankfurt, but he lives outside the city. He ¹..... and takes the train to Frankfurt. He ²..... work at 7.30 a.m. Three times a week he ³..... He ⁴..... in the canteen. In the afternoon ⁵..... He ⁶..... at 4.00 p.m. twice a week. He ⁷..... after work.

6.5 Complete the article about Peter Schmidt with information from the chart in 6.4.

7 Culture Focus

Look at the information in the table. Then make notes about your country or company and another country or company you know well.

	UK
Start work before 8.00 a.m.	not very often
Have lunch in a pub	sometimes
Have a sandwich at the desk	sometimes
Take work home	managers often; other staff sometimes
Go out with colleagues after work	often

8 Output

8.1 Think about a typical week at your work. Make notes of any new words.

8.2 Work with a partner and have a conversation about your routines.

Roles	You are yourselves.
Relationship	You know each other, but not very well.
Place	In a social setting, like a bar or restaurant, after a business meeting.

City Profiles

1 Preview

You plan to go on a business trip to a new city.

What do you want to know about that place?

2 Wordwork

2.1 Match the products and industries.

Example: 1 = f

Products	Industries
1 ships/ferries	a) textiles
2 tinned fruit/ vegetables	b) pharmaceuticals
	c) chemicals
3 beer	d) electronics
4 plastics	e) engineering
5 cloth	f) shipbuilding
6 TVs and radios	g) food processing
7 fruit and vegetables	h) brewing
	i) agriculture
8 engines	
9 medicines	

2.2 Make a list of three important industries in your region or city.

2.3 Complete this sentence about your region or city.

In . . . . . , the main industries are
. . . . . , ... and . . . . . .

3 Language Focus

Interconsult is an international organisation which helps companies to do business in other countries. Marianne Boucher works in their Brussels office.

Marianne telephones two people for information about Bratislava, the capital city of Slovakia.

3.1 🖳 Listen and complete the table.

CITY Bratislava

1 Industries
   a) electronics ☐   d) shipbuilding ☐   g) chemicals ☐
   b) pharmaceuticals ☐   e) engineering ☐   h) food processing ☐
   c) textiles ☐   f) brewing ☐   i) agriculture ☐

2 International companies? Yes ☐   No ☐

3 Company working hours from ..... to .....

4 Transport: underground? Yes ☐   No ☐

5 Costs
   a) a hotel room .....
   b) to rent a car .....

3.2 🖳 Listen again. What questions does she ask about

1 the main industries?
2 international companies?
3 the working hours of companies?
4 the average cost of a hotel room?
5 an underground?
6 car rental?

LANGUAGE SUMMARY

Yes/No questions

QUESTIONS	ANSWERS
Is there an underground?	No, **there isn't.**
Are there any international companies?	Yes, **there are.**

Open questions

What are	the main industries?
	the working hours of companies?

What's the average cost of a hotel room?
How much does it cost to rent a car?

1 Which question do we use with bank?
 a) Are there any . . . . . ?
 b) Is there a . . . . . ?
2 Which question do we use with cinemas?
 a) Are there any . . . . . ?
 b) Is there a . . . . . ?

4 Numberwork

4.1 Which countries use these currencies?

Example: 1 = UK

Countries	Currencies
1	pound sterling (£)
2	US dollar ($)
3	Deutschmark (DM)
4	yen (Y)
5	peseta (pta)
6	lira (L)

4.2 List other countries and currencies you know.

NUMBERWORK SUMMARY

You see	You say
£80	eighty pounds
DM3,000	three thousand Deutschmarks
pta13,000	thirteen thousand pesetas
Y1,200	one thousand two hundred yen
L35,000	thirty-five thousand lire
$19.50	nineteen dollars and fifty cents
£10.20	ten pounds twenty

4.3 How do you say these prices?

1 £56	3 Y450	5 pta1,800	7 $94.50
2 $280	4 DM1,500	6 L50,000	8 £35.25

5 Practice

5.1 Make questions. Ask about these points.

1 a hotel room	4 eat in a good restaurant
2 rent a car	5 take a taxi to the airport
3 a meal with wine	6 a taxi ride

Models
What's the average cost of a hotel room?
How much does it cost to rent a car?

5.2 Work with a partner.
Student A: Look at page 111.
Student B: Ask your partner questions about costs in Munich and London. Complete the table.

	Hotel	To rent a car
Munich		
London		
New York	$270	$100 a day
Madrid	pta18,000	pta9,000 a day

5.3 Now answer your partner's questions about costs in New York and Madrid.

5.4 Ask your partner questions about the working hours of companies and banks in Belgium. Complete the table.

Working hours in Belgium	
Companies	
Banks	
Shops	Mon–Thurs and Sat: 9.15 a.m.– 6.00 p.m. Fri: 9.15 a.m.–9.00 p.m.
Government offices	Mon–Fri: 9.00 a.m.–12.00 and 2.00 p.m.–5.00 p.m.

5.5 Now answer your partner's questions about shops and government offices.

5.6 Work with a partner. Ask and answer questions about your towns or cities. Ask about these points.

1 five star hotels
2 airport
3 underground
4 big department stores
5 English language cinemas
6 theatre

Models
A Is there . . . . . ?
B Yes, there is./No, there isn't.
A Are there . . . . . ?
B Yes, there are./No, there aren't.

6 Tactics Focus

Marianne Boucher phones Akira Nakatane at Interbank in London for some information about working hours and hotel costs in Japan.

6.1 🔲 Listen to their conversation and answer the questions.

1 Does Mr Nakatane tell her
 a) most companies work from 9.00 to 5.00?
 b) most companies work from 9.00 to 6.00?
2 Does Mr Nakatane tell her
 a) a good hotel costs Y15,000?
 b) hotels cost from Y15,000 to Y30,000?

6.2 What are the missing words in the conversations?

6.3 🔲 Listen again. Are your words the same as the words on the cassette?

TACTICS SUMMARY

When people give long or difficult answers, check you really understand.
So about Y15,000 for a good hotel?

When people understand you, tell them.
Yes, that's right.

When people don't understand you, correct them and give the right information again.
No, that's not quite right. For a good hotel you pay about Y30,000.

---

7 Practice

Work with a partner. Ask and answer questions about costs in your cities or towns. Ask about these points.

1 a hotel room
2 a meal in a good restaurant
3 a theatre ticket
4 a taxi to the airport

8 Output

8.1 Work in groups of three. A and B ask and answer questions about cities. C checks the information and makes notes.
Student A: Look at page 111.
Student C: Look at page 113.
Student B: Answer A's questions about Copenhagen.

	Copenhagen
Office working hours	8.30 to 4.30
Underground?	no
Cost of hotel room	1,000 kroner
Cost of car rental	650 kroner a day
Industries	engineering, textiles

8.2 Now ask for the same information about Amsterdam.

7

Country Profiles

1 Preview

Your organisation plans to open an office in another country.

What information do you want about that country?

2 Language Focus

Stanley Tam, a Hong Kong businessman, plans to open an office in Belgium.

2.1 Read this fax from Marianne Boucher of Interconsult in Brussels. What questions do you think Stanley Tam asked her?

Interconsult

facsimile

To	Stanley Tam
From	Marianne Boucher
Subject	Your fax of 23 September

Thank you for your fax asking for information about Belgium. Here are the answers to your questions:

a) There are 10 million people in Belgium.
b) The inflation rate is about 3% at the moment.
c) There are two official languages – French and Flemish. Many people speak English in big companies.
d) The normal working week is 38 to 40 hours.
e) The minimum holiday is 20 days per year.

2.2 Match Stanley's questions and Marianne's answers.

1 How many hours do people work?
2 What's the inflation rate?
3 What language do people speak at work?
4 How much holiday do people get?
5 What's the population?

3 Wordwork

3.1 Complete this list.

Countries	Languages/ Nationalities	Countries	Languages/ Nationalities
Japan	Japanese	Italy	Italian
China	. . . . .	Hungary	. . . . .
Portugal	. . . . .	Germany	. . . . .
Sweden	Swedish	Korea	. . . . .
Poland	. . . . .	Greece	Greek
Ireland	. . . . .	France	. . . . .
Spain	. . . . .	Holland	. . . . .

3.2 Listen and underline the stressed syllable in the words in 3.1.

Example: Ja**pan**   Japa**nese**

3.3 What languages do people speak in your country

1 at home?
2 at work?
3 in different regions?

4 Numberwork

4.1 📼 Listen and repeat these numbers.

1	8%	3	25%	5	5.5%	7	4.6m
2	17%	4	1.1%	6	2.5m	8	7.2bn

4.2 Answer these questions about your country.

1 What's the inflation rate?
2 What's the population?
3 What's the unemployment rate?
4 What's the unemployment figure?

5 Practice

5.1 Make questions with how much and how many.

Example: How much beer do they produce?
How many litres of beer do they produce?

1 beer/litres of beer (produce)
2 chocolate/boxes of chocolates (sell)
3 wine/bottles of wine (export)
4 holiday/weeks of holiday (get)
5 fruit/tonnes of apples (grow)
6 oil/barrels of oil (import)

5.2 Here are some answers about Ireland. What are the questions?

1 Gaelic and English.
2 4%.
3 3.5 million.
4 40 hours a week.
5 Agriculture, food processing and electronics.
6 4 or 5 weeks a year.

6 Writing

6.1 Read this fax from Marianne Boucher.

facsimile

To   The Costa Rican Embassy
From   Marianne Boucher
Subject Costa Rica

Could you give me some information?

a) What's the population of Costa Rica?
b) What languages do people speak?
c) What are the main industries?
d) What does the country export?

6.2 Write a fax to Marianne Boucher, answering her questions. Use this information.

bananas, coffee, sugar	3 million textiles, food processing, tourism	Spanish, and English at work in some companies

LEARNING TIP

Look at the list. When you read these things in your own language, do you
1 read every word?
2 read quickly to find the information you need, then read a part in detail?

	1	2
A newspaper	☐	☐
A telephone book	☐	☐
A letter from a customer	☐	☐
A contract to buy or rent a house	☐	☐
A computer manual	☐	☐

■ Reading in English is like reading in your own language. Sometimes it is necessary to read every word. But very often you can read quickly to find the information you need. Then you can read that part in detail.

7 Reading

This extract is from a guide for companies planning to start a business in Greece.

7.1 Find information about these points.

the population
the inflation rate
the main industries
the language
the working week

7.2 Match each picture to one paragraph.

7.3 Choose a title for each paragraph.

8 Output

8.1 Choose a country you know well. Make notes about it.

Country
Population
Inflation rate
Main industries
Working week
Minimum holiday
Languages

8.2 Work with a partner. Have a conversation about the countries you know.

Greece

FACTS AND FIGURES

Population 10 million
Capital Athens
Language Greek
Unemployment 8%

Inflation 15%
Currency Drachma
Political system Republic

- **Greece** offers an attractive, low-cost location for foreign companies.

1 —
- **Greece** has major agricultural and food-processing industries. It grows and exports vegetables and fruit, mainly to the Middle East and Europe. **Greece** is also a big exporter of tinned olives, tomatoes and other vegetables. Wine is another important export, especially the famous wine Retsina.

2 —
- Tourism is an important source of foreign currency, with about 8 million visitors a year. Tourism is especially important for the economy of the Greek islands.

3 —
- The normal working day is 8 hours and there is a 40-hour working week. There are 12 official public holidays. The minimum holiday is 20 days a year.

4 —
- **Greece** is a major exporter of cement for the construction industry. It exports 50% of its production to countries such as the UK, the USA and Saudi Arabia. Other industries are textiles, chemicals and shipbuilding. Today around 50% of big manufacturing companies are in the Athens area.

A

B

8

Entertaining

1 Preview

The people in the picture are at a conference. Two of them are colleagues. The other one works for another company.

What are they talking about? What are they saying?

2 Language Focus

Jane, Peter and Eva work for PBX. They are at a sales conference.

2.1 📟 Listen to their conversation. Are these sentences true or false?

	True	False
1 Peter knows Eva.	☐	☐
2 Jane offers drinks to Peter and Eva.	☐	☐
3 Eva doesn't want a drink.	☐	☐
4 Jane and Eva like Spanish wine.	☐	☐

2.2 Complete the conversation with these sentences.

a) No, thanks. I'm fine.
b) What kind of red wine would you like?
c) Yes, please. I'd like a glass of red wine.
d) Could we have two glasses of red wine, please?
e) Would you like another drink?
f) Yes, I do.
g) Do you like Spanish wine, Eva?

JANE	Can I get you a drink, Eva?
EVA	[1].....
JANE	OK. What about you Peter? [2].....
PETER	[3].....
JANE	Excuse me. [4].....
BARMAN	Certainly. [5].....
JANE	Do you have any Spanish wine?
BARMAN	Yes, we have a very good *Rioja*.
JANE	That's fine for me. [6].....
EVA	[7].....

2.3 📟 Listen again. Is your conversation the same as the conversation on the cassette?

LANGUAGE SUMMARY

Offering drinks

| Can I get you | a drink? |
| Would you like | another drink? |

Accepting or declining drinks
Yes, please. I'd like a glass of red wine.
No, thanks. I'm fine.

Ordering from the bar

| Could we have two glasses of | red wine, | please? |
| | orange juice, | |

Questions
What kind of wine would you like?
Do you like Spanish wine?

CHECK!

You want to know what a person wants to drink. Which question do you ask?
1 What do you like?
2 What would you like?

3 Practice

3.1 Choose the correct answer to these questions.

1 Do you like champagne?
   a) Yes, I do.
   b) Yes, I would.
2 Would you like another glass of champagne?
   a) No, thanks. I'm fine.
   b) No, I don't.
3 What kind of champagne do you like?
   a) Bollinger.
   b) Yes, please.
4 What kind of champagne would you like?
   a) Yes, I would.
   b) Bollinger, please.

3.2 Work in groups of three and have conversations. Use the drinks list. Take turns to be the host, the guest and the waiter or waitress.

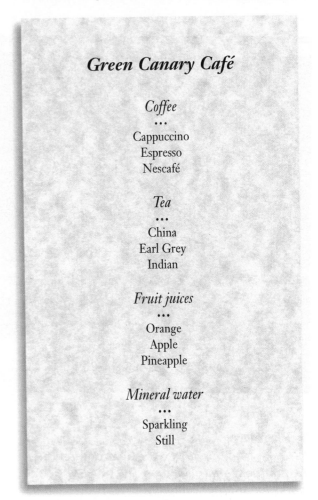

Green Canary Café

Coffee
...
Cappuccino
Espresso
Nescafé

Tea
...
China
Earl Grey
Indian

Fruit juices
...
Orange
Apple
Pineapple

Mineral water
...
Sparkling
Still

4 Conversation Focus

4.1 ▭ Listen to two conversations between Peter and Eva. Match the conversations and the pictures.

Conversation 1   Picture ☐
Conversation 2   Picture ☐

A   B

4.2 ▣ **Read the first conversation and listen again to the second conversation. What are the differences?**

PETER What do you do, Eva?

EVA I'm a sales representative in the Swedish subsidiary.

PETER Where exactly do you work?

EVA I work in the Stockholm office.

PETER I think I know some of the people there. Is Stig Larsson still responsible for sales in Stockholm?

EVA No, Stig's in Gothenburg now.

PETER Who's your new boss?

EVA It's Agnes Miklos.

PETER I don't know her. Where's she from?

EVA She's from Hungary.

CONVERSATION SUMMARY

In conversations it is important to sound friendly and interested. Here are some ideas to help you.

■ Mix Yes/No questions and open questions.

■ Repeat some of the information the other person gives you.

■ Use short questions (Oh, do you?/Oh, are you?) to show you are interested.

■ Give extra information when you answer questions.

5 Practice

5.1 Work with a partner and have conversations. Use these sentences.

1 I work for Keatings.
2 I'm from Spain.
3 I live in France.
4 I'm Danish.
5 I work for a publishing company.
6 I'm a sales representative.

Models

A I work for Keatings.

B Oh, do you? What exactly do you do?/Keatings. What do you do there?

A I'm from Spain.

B Oh, are you? Where in Spain are you from?/ Spain. Where exactly are you from?

5.2 How can you make this conversation sound more friendly?

MARGARETE WUNDER What do you do?

CHRISTINE SAVILLE I work for Park and Moss.

MARGARETE WUNDER What exactly do you do?

CHRISTINE SAVILLE I'm a tax consultant.

MARGARETE WUNDER Where do you work?

CHRISTINE SAVILLE In the Head Office in London.

MARGARETE WUNDER Do you know Wolfgang Binder? He works for Park and Moss in Germany.

CHRISTINE SAVILLE Yes, I do.

6 Culture Focus

Look at the table. Then think about the situation in your country and another country you know well.

In bars in the UK...	
... people usually order a) at the table. b) at the bar.	✗ ✓
... people usually pay a) when they get their drinks. b) when they leave the bar.	✓ ✗
... people usually a) leave a tip for the bar staff. b) keep the change.	✗ ✓

7 Output

Work in groups of three and have a conversation.

Roles	You choose! Decide who you are, who you work for, what you do and where you live.
Relationships	A knows B and C. B and C do not know each other.
Place	In a bar at the end of the first day of a conference.

Conversation Plan

A Introduce B and C. Offer them drinks.

B AND C Accept drinks. Start a conversation with each other.

A New Job

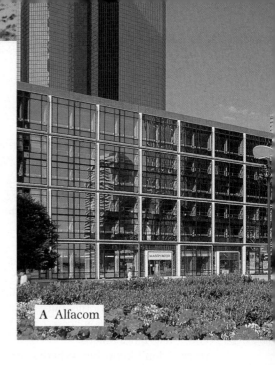

A Alfacom

1 Writing

1.1 Look at the information about a company called Alfacom in the table. Complete these sentences.

1 They're in the . . . . . business.
2 They're based in . . . . . .
3 They have . . . . . employees in Paris.
4 The employees get three weeks . . . . . .
5 . . . . . is a sports centre.

1.2 You want the same information about Borelec. What questions can you ask? Complete the fax.

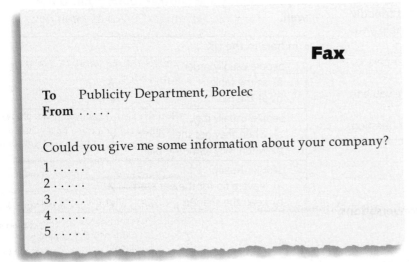

Fax

To   Publicity Department, Borelec
From . . . . .

Could you give me some information about your company?

1 . . . . .
2 . . . . .
3 . . . . .
4 . . . . .
5 . . . . .

	A Alfacom
Business	computer hardware
Based in	La Défense, Paris
Employees	700 in Paris, 12,000 in the world
Holiday	3 weeks per year
Facilities – Sports centre	yes

2 Reading

Student A: Look at page 111.
Student B: Your teacher will give you a fax from Borelec. Read the fax and complete part B of the table.

3 Speaking

3.1 Ask your partner about Diamond Electro and complete part D of the table.

3.2 Answer your partner's questions about Comex.

B Borelec   C Comex   D Diamond Electro

	B Borelec	C Comex	D Diamond Electro
		computer games	
		Strasbourg	
		45 in Strasbourg only	
		5 weeks per year	
		no	

4 Reading

Complete part A of the table below with this information about Marie Dupuy.

a job in a big company
Sales Manager for a small company based in Paris
to move from Paris
to use her Italian
selling personal computers

French and Italian
sports
French
modern offices

		A Marie Dupuy	B Jean-Luc Pons
1	Nationality		
2	Present job		
3	Responsible for		
4	Languages		
5	He/she wants		
6	He/she likes		

5 Listening

🎧 **Listen to an interview with Jean-Luc Pons and complete part B of the table.**

6 Output

Alfacom, Borelec, Comex and Diamond Electro all need new Sales Managers.

6.1 Match the descriptions and the companies.

1 **Sales Manager (France and Germany)**
This small electronics company, based in Paris, needs a new Sales Manager to sell its products in France and Germany.

2 **Sales Manager (Southern Europe)**
This international company, based in Nice, needs a new Sales Manager to sell its electronic products in southern Europe (especially Italy and Spain).

3 **Sales Manager (Europe)**
This small company needs a new Sales Manager who speaks three languages to sell its computer games all over Europe.

4 **Sales Manager for France**
This Paris-based company needs a new Sales Manager to sell its computer products all over France.

6.2 Work in groups. Choose one of the jobs in 6.1 for Marie Dupuy and one for Jean-Luc Pons. What are your reasons?

9

Career Development

1 Preview

Think about important events in the last five years. Talk about your life, your company and your country.

2 Wordwork

2.1 Match the verbs and their meanings.

Example: 1 = d

Verbs	Meanings
1 join	a) You move to a different job or place, but in the same organisation.
2 retire	
3 resign	b) You go to another location or another company in a different place.
4 transfer	
5 stay	c) You leave the company because you are 65.
6 move	d) You start to work for an organisation.
	e) You leave your organisation because you want to.
	f) You don't leave your organisation.

2.2 Put these verbs in the table.

change   move   transfer   finish   start   resign
join   stay   retire

Changes	
No changes	
The start	
The end	

Tim Waterstone

BUSINESSMAN AND BOOKSELLER

Tim Waterstone was born in the south of England in 1939. He studied at Cambridge University. When he finished his studies he wasn't sure what to do, but he didn't want to stay in England. So he joined a small company of tea traders in India and he worked there from

3 Language Focus A

Read the article about Tim Waterstone and then complete the time line.

Date	Event
	was born
	worked for a company of tea traders in India
1965	
	moved to WH Smith
	started his own company
1989	

1962 to 1964. It was his first job and he was very happy there. He returned to England and the following year he started a new job in the Marketing Department of Allied Lyons. Some years later he changed company and moved to WH Smith, a chain of booksellers. He was responsible for their American division. In 1982 he started his own company, Waterstone and Co. He opened bookshops all over the UK. They were very successful and the company expanded rapidly. In 1989 he decided to sell his company. WH Smith agreed to pay £42 million for it. ■

LANGUAGE SUMMARY A

Simple past: verb be
Tim Waterstone's company **was** successful.
The bookshops **were** successful.
He **wasn't** sure what to do.

Simple past: regular verbs
He **worked** in India from 1962 to 1964.
He **lived** there for two years.
In 1982 he **started** his own company.
He **didn't stay** in England.

CHECK!

1 **How do you make the simple past of regular verbs?**
2 **What is the simple past of these verbs?**
retire   stay   resign   transfer

4 Speechwork

📟 **When you add ed to a verb you can make three sounds. Listen. Do you hear sound 1, sound 2 or sound 3?**

		1	2	3
1	finished	☐	☑	☐
2	joined	☐	☐	☐
3	started	☐	☐	☐
4	returned	☐	☐	☐
5	worked	☐	☐	☐
6	opened	☐	☐	☐
7	transferred	☐	☐	☐
8	changed	☐	☐	☐

5 Numberwork

5.1 Find five dates in the article about Tim Waterstone. How do you say the years?

NUMBERWORK SUMMARY

You see	You say
1901	nineteen oh one
1918	nineteen eighteen
1962	nineteen sixty-two
1989	nineteen eighty-nine
1990	nineteen ninety

5.2 How do you say these years?

1 1905   3 1978   5 1995
2 1916   4 1980

6 Practice

6.1 Look at the time line in 3 and talk about Tim Waterstone's career.

6.2 📟 Listen to an interview about Tim Waterstone's career. There are seven mistakes. What are they? Make sentences like this.

Examples: 1 He wasn't born in 1949. He was born in 1939.

2 He didn't stay in India for four years. He stayed there for two years.

7 Language Focus B

David Bellan works for Astral, an international oil company.

7.1 📼 **Listen to an interview about his career development at Astral. What four jobs did he do?**

7.2 Match words from A and B to make complete questions.

Example: 1 = b

A	B
1 Was	a) you stay?
2 Were	b) it your first job?
3 What did	c) you enjoy the job?
4 Did	d) your next job?
5 What was	e) your responsibilities at Astral very different?
6 How long did	f) you do there?

7.3 📼 **Listen again. Are your questions the same as the questions on the cassette?**

LANGUAGE SUMMARY B

Simple past questions: verb **be**
Was the job interesting?
Were the responsibilities different?

What	**was** your first/next job?
	were your responsibilities?

Simple past questions
Did you **enjoy** the job?
What **did** you **do** next?
How long **did** you **stay** there?

CHECK!

1 **How do you make a question in the simple past?**
2 **Correct these questions.**
   a) Did you enjoyed the film?
   b) Did the job be interesting?
   c) How long you were there?

8 Practice

8.1 Complete this conversation with questions from Language Summary B.

INTERVIEWER	So you finished your studies in 1990. 1 . . . .
KEN TARLINGTON	I joined Wilcox Australia. I worked there as a sales representative.
INTERVIEWER	2 . . . .
KEN TARLINGTON	Yes, very much. It was a very interesting job with a lot of travel.
INTERVIEWER	3 . . . .
KEN TARLINGTON	I changed company and moved to Cometek, another construction company, but in Sydney.
INTERVIEWER	4 . . . .
KEN TARLINGTON	I was responsible for sales.
INTERVIEWER	5 . . . .
KEN TARLINGTON	For two years. Then I transferred to their subsidiary in Singapore. That was last year.

8.2 Work with a partner.
Student A: Look at page 112.
Student B: Jim Lake works for Wilcox International. Ask and answer questions about his career. Complete the table. A starts.

	Responsibilities	Dates
Wilcox Canada	Computer Operator	
Wilcox Malaysia		1990–92
Wilcox Japan	Business Support Manager	

9 Output

9.1 Work with a partner. Find out about his or her career development. Make notes on important dates and events.

9.2 Give a short presentation about your partner's career development.

Company History

1 VW launched the Beetle

2 Work began on the Channel Tunnel

3 Disney built a resort near Paris

1 Preview

Do you know when these events happened?

2 Wordwork

Which verbs and nouns can go together?

Verbs	Nouns
1 build	a) a subsidiary
2 launch	b) the production of oil
3 merge	c) an assembly plant
4 set up	d) with other companies
5 begin	e) another company
6 take over	f) a new product

3 Language Focus

4 BMW took over Rover

3.1 Read this article about Saab-Scania.

The Road to Success

The first Scania truck left the factory 93 years ago. In 1911, Scania merged with Vabis, another truck manufacturer. Thirteen years later the new company shut Scania's original factory in Malmö, but kept the factory in Sodertalje, near Stockholm. During the Second World War, Scania-Vabis made trucks for the Swedish army. Then in 1957 Scania-Vabis set up a subsidiary in Brazil. This gave Scania-Vabis its first overseas market. In 1964 the company chose Zwolle in the Netherlands for its first assembly plant in the EC. In 1969 Saab merged with Scania-Vabis and the old company became a division of Saab-Scania. They continued to expand and, in 1976, set up a subsidiary in Argentina. In 1984 they launched a new generation of trucks. The following year they began to sell in the North American market. In 1989 Saab-Scania won the award for 'truck of the year'. Three years ago Saab-Scania opened a factory in France. Today Scania is active in over a hundred markets around the world. ■

3.2 Read the article again and find the simple past of these verbs.

1 become   4 give   7 leave   10 set up
2 begin   5 keep   8 make   11 shut
3 choose   6 launch   9 merge   12 win

CHECK!

1 Which verbs have irregular endings?
2 Which irregular verbs don't change their spelling?
3 When did the first Scania truck leave the factory – 1993 or 1902?

3.3 Match the questions and answers.

Example: 1 = f

Questions	Answers
1 When did Scania merge with Vabis?	a) In the Netherlands.
2 Did the company shut the plant in Malmö?	b) For 58 years.
3 When did they open a subsidiary in Brazil?	c) In 1957.
4 Where did they set up their plant in the EC?	d) Yes, it did.
5 How long did they keep the name Scania-Vabis?	e) No, it didn't.
6 Did Scania merge with Volvo?	f) In 1911.

LANGUAGE SUMMARY

Simple past: irregular verbs
The first truck **left** the factory 93 years ago.
They **set up** a subsidiary in 1957.
In 1985 they **began** to sell in the North American market.

Yes/No questions: simple past

QUESTIONS		ANSWERS
Did Scania	**merge** with Volvo?	No, they **didn't**.
	win an award?	Yes, they **did**.

Open questions: simple past

When	did they	**begin** to sell in the US?
Where		**set up** in the EC?

Negatives: simple past
They **didn't keep** the name Scania-Vabis after the merger.

---

4 Practice

The time line shows the important events in the development of Saab-Scania.

Date	Event
1902	The first Scania truck leaves the factory.
1911	Scania merges with Vabis.
1957	Scania sets up a subsidiary in Brazil.
1964	The company chooses the Netherlands for its first assembly plant in the EC.
1969	Saab merges with Scania-Vabis.
1976	Saab-Scania sets up a subsidiary in Argentina.
1984	Saab-Scania launches a new generation of trucks.
1989	Saab-Scania wins an award.
1992	Saab-Scania opens a factory in France.

4.1 Work with a partner. Ask and answer questions about the development of Scania.

Model
A When did Scania set up a subsidiary in Brazil?
B In 1957.

4.2 When did the events in the table happen? Make sentences with ago.

Example: The first truck left the factory ..... years ago.

4.3 Talk about business events in your country. Use verbs from 2.

5 Tactics Focus

A journalist for a business magazine is interviewing Enrique Bernat, Managing Director of Chupa Chups, a Spanish confectionery company.

5.1 🖭 Listen and complete these sentences.

1 He took over from his father in . . . . . .
   a) 1955   b) 1957
2 He built the factory in France in . . . . . .
   a) 1967   b) 1969
3 The other foreign factory is in . . . . . .
   a) Japan   b) Russia
4 Sales to Japan were . . . . . .
   a) $20m   b) $7m

5.2 🖭 What does the journalist say? Listen again and find examples where she

1 asks Enrique Bernat for information again.
2 repeats his answers to check she really understands.

TACTICS SUMMARY

When you want to be really sure you have the right information, ask again.
Sorry, I didn't catch that. When did you open the factory?
Sorry, what was the sales figure?

When the other person gives you the information again, you can repeat it to check.
1969. I see.
$20 million. OK.

6 Practice

6.1 You want somebody to give you this information again. What questions can you ask?

                    the event   the date
Alba Fashions opened an office in Hong Kong in 1994.
                    the location

6.2 Work with a partner and have a conversation about Scania. Use the information in the time line in 4.

Model
A When did Scania start to make trucks?
B I think it was in 1902.
A Sorry, what was the date?
B 1902.
A 1902. OK.

7 Speechwork

🖭 **Listen and underline the main stress in the answers.**

Model
INTERVIEWER So you took over the family business in 1955?
INTERVIEWEE No, it was in 195*7*.

1 INTERVIEWER So you took over the family business in 1955?
   INTERVIEWEE No, it was in 1957.
2 INTERVIEWER So you built the new plant in France?
   INTERVIEWEE No, we built it in Spain.
3 INTERVIEWER So you built the plant in Spain in 1994?
   INTERVIEWEE No, we built it in 1995.
4 INTERVIEWER So you sold 20,000 cars in 1994?
   INTERVIEWEE No, we sold 30,000.

8 Output

8.1 Prepare a time line to show the development of your organisation.

8.2 Work with a partner. Explain your time line to him or her. He/she asks questions and checks the important events and dates.

Past Performance

1 Preview

What changes did you see in your country in the late 80s and the early 90s? Talk about these points.

public transport traffic
speed limits on the roads
imports of foreign cars
petrol prices

2 Wordwork

2.1 Look at these verbs. They are useful for describing a graph.

go up   increase
decrease   remain constant
fall   go down
rise   stay at the same level

Complete the table with the correct verbs.

1 ↗	
2 →	
3 ↘	

2.2 What is the simple past of these verbs? Complete the table.

Simple past
decrease
fall
go up/down
increase
remain
stay

3 Language Focus

A presenter describes what happened to car production in the three countries in these graphs.

3.1 ▭ Listen and match each description with one of the graphs.

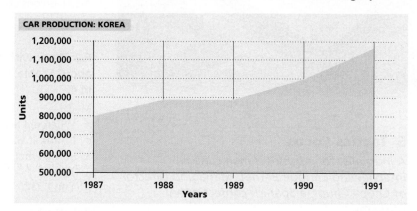

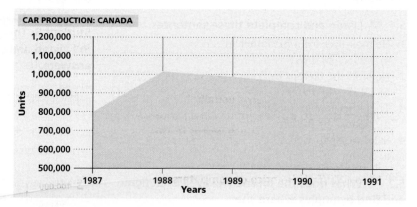

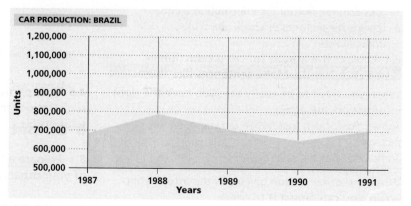

3.2 What happened to production in the three countries? Complete the table.

	Verb	Adverb	Amount/new level
1	. . . . . fell	sharply steadily	to over 1 million . . . . .
2	rose decreased	– . . . . . slightly	. . . . . to 670,000 . . . . .
3	increased . . . . . went up	. . . . . – –	– at the same level . . . . .

LANGUAGE SUMMARY

Simple past

Production	went up increased rose	slightly. steadily. sharply.
Output	went down decreased fell	slightly. steadily. sharply.

Production remained constant.
Output stayed at the same level.

Production fell	from 800,000 to 700,000 cars. by 100,000 cars.

CHECK!

1 **What ending do adverbs usually have?**
2 **Where do you put an adverb in a sentence?**
3 **Make sentences. Put these words in the correct order.**
   a) petrol prices/up/steadily/went.
   b) rapidly/fell/the price of computers.

4 Practice

4.1 Look at the graphs for car production in Korea and Canada. Make sentences like these.

Examples:
                          time   verb   adverb
In 1988 production went up slightly.
Production went up slightly in 1988.
                                   verb   adverb   time

4.2 Complete the reports on car production in Korea and Canada with from, to or by.

Korea

In 1988 car production rose slightly [1]. . . . . about 900,000 cars, and it stayed at this level for a year. [2]. . . . . 1989 [3]. . . . . 1991 production rose again [4]. . . . . 300,000 cars [5]. . . . . nearly 1.2 million.

Canada

Car production in Canada increased [1]. . . . . just over 800,000 in 1987 to just over one million in 1988. For the next three years production fell [2]. . . . . about 45,000 cars each year [3]. . . . . 900,000 in 1991.

4.3 Write a short report on car production in Brazil. Use the information in 3.1.

4.4 Work with a partner.
Student A: Look at page 112.
Student B: This graph shows new car registrations in Finland. Describe it to your partner. He/she draws your graph.

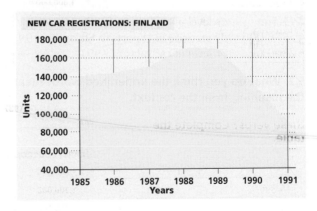

NEW CAR REGISTRATIONS: FINLAND

Units / Years

4.5 Your partner has information about new car registrations in Norway. Add the information to your graph.

Korean Car Makers Look To Europe

Export drive for Korean cars

SALLY COLMAN

In 1991 Korean car sales rose by 15% to 1.5m units, but profits for Hyundai, Kia and Daewoo fell. Profits were low because of the high cost of modernising and building car factories. In the early 90s, the home market accounted for 74% of Korean car makers' sales. But home sales in the early 90s did not increase very much because of new taxes and high petrol prices.

In 1988, a very good year, exports of Korean cars reached a <u>peak</u> of 576,000. At that time the main export market was the US. But at the end of the 80s sales to the US <u>dropped</u> sharply and Korean exports fell to a low of 347,000 in 1990. The export market <u>declined</u> because of problems in the US economy and also because the quality of Korean cars was not very good at that time. The decrease in exports to the US continued in the early 90s, but exports to Europe, the Middle East and Latin America started to increase. In 1992 exports to Europe <u>grew</u> by over 130% and exports to the Middle East rose by 300%.

5 Reading

5.1 Read the report on Korean cars. The numbers on the left are from the report. Find each number in the report and match it with one of the events on the right.

Example: 1 = d

Numbers		Events
1	130%	a) level of exports in 1988
2	347,000	b) increase in exports to the Middle East in 1992
3	1.5m	c) level of exports in 1990
4	576,000	d) increase in exports to Europe in 1992
5	300%	e) level of car sales in 1991

5.2 What do you think the underlined words mean? Try to guess the meaning from the context.

6 Output

6.1 Choose one of the topics from the Preview on page 38. Draw a graph to show what happened in your country.

6.2 Work with a partner. Describe your graph to him or her.

6.3 Now draw the graph your partner describes.

12

Small Talk

1 Preview

What do you say to people in these situations?

1 A supplier comes to visit you. The last time you saw him was a month ago.
2 You meet a colleague in the company restaurant. You know she was at a sales conference last week.
3 You go to visit a client. You know he was on holiday two weeks ago.

2 Language Focus

Jane works for PBX in Vancouver, Canada. Terry works for an advertising agency.

2.1 ▣ Listen to their conversation and answer these questions.

1 Do Terry and Jane know each other?
2 Does Terry know where Jane was last week?

2.2 Match words from A and B to make complete sentences.

Example: 1 = e

A	B
1 It's nice	a) city.
2 How are	b) you?
3 How was	c) of Toronto?
4 What did you think	d) very good.
5 The weather wasn't	e) to see you again.
6 It's a very attractive	f) the sales conference.

2.3 ▣ Listen again. Are your sentences the same as the sentences on the cassette?

LANGUAGE SUMMARY

Greeting people you know

QUESTIONS	ANSWERS
	I'm fine.
How are you?	Fine, thanks.
	Very well, thanks.
It's nice to see you again.	

Questions
How was the sales conference?
What did you think of Toronto?

Describing
The conference was very interesting.
The weather wasn't very good.
It's a very attractive city.

3 Speechwork

▣ Listen to these sentences from the conversation in 2.1 and underline the stressed syllables.

Example: It's <u>nice</u> to <u>see</u> you a<u>gain</u>.
How <u>are</u> you?

1 It's nice to see you again. How are you?
2 I'm fine. How are you?
3 Fine, thanks.
4 The weather wasn't very good, but it's a very attractive city.

4 Practice

Look again at the Preview. Work with a partner and have a conversation for each situation.

5 Wordwork

5.1 Match the adjectives with the nouns they can describe.

Adjectives	Nouns
1 comfortable	a) a film
2 wonderful	b) the weather
3 attractive	c) food/a meal
4 good	d) a hotel
5 nice	e) people
6 delicious	f) a holiday
7 excellent	g) a conference
8 interesting	h) a beach
	i) a city

Many English adjectives can describe a range of feelings like this.

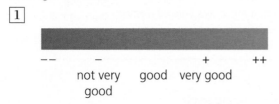

```
 --      -            +        ++
     not very   good   very good
       good
```

But some adjectives can describe only very strong feelings like this.

```
 --                              ++
 terrible                   excellent
 disgusting                 delicious
```

5.2 Look again at the adjectives in 5.1. Are they the first kind (1) or the second kind (2)?

A

B

5.3 Look at the cartoons. Which conversation is more appropriate?

5.4 Work with a partner and have conversations. Ask about these points.

1 have a meal in a hotel   4 go on holiday
2 stay in a hotel   5 go to a conference
3 see a film

Model
A When did you last have a meal in a hotel?
B . . . . . .
A How was the meal?
B . . . . . .

6 Conversation Focus

6.1 Listen to two conversations and answer these questions.

In which conversation do the people
1 know the same people?
2 know the same places?

6.2 What questions did the people ask about

1 the sales conference?   4 Knossos?
2 Stig Larsson?   5 the food in Crete?
3 Christine's holiday?

CONVERSATION SUMMARY

When you make small talk with people you know, ask about things you know they did between your last meeting and this meeting.

■ You can ask general questions about a holiday, training course, conference or business trip.
How was the holiday?
What did you think of the food in Crete?

■ If you know the place or people, you can also ask for specific information.
Was Stig Larsson there?
Did you go to Knossos?

7 Practice

7.1 What questions can you ask in these situations?

1 You know your client was in Japan on business last week. You don't know where in Japan he went.

2 Your friend was on holiday in Japan last month. She planned to go to Kyoto, but you're not sure if she went there.

3 A colleague visited your Japanese subsidiary last week. A friend of yours, Ann Clay, works there.

4 You visit a supplier in Tokyo. You know he is interested in cinema and that there was a film festival in Tokyo last week.

7.2 Work with a partner and have conversations. Use the role cards your teacher gives you.

8 Culture Focus

How important is small talk when you do business? Look at the table. Then think about the situation in your country and another country you know well.

	UK	Finland
When do people make small talk?	before a meeting	after a meeting
How important is small talk?	important	not very important
What do people like talking about?	people they both know; places they both know; hobbies; the weather; the cost of living	people they both know; places they both know; sports; the countryside; the cost of living
What don't people talk about very much?	their salaries; their families; food	their salaries; the weather; political opinions

9 Output

9.1 Think about your last holiday or business trip. Where did you go? What did you do, see, eat, visit?

9.2 Work with a partner. Make small talk about your last holiday or business trip.

Roles	You choose (e.g. client and supplier, or colleagues from the same company but different departments).
Relationship	You know each other.
Place	In a bar or restaurant, or in your office before a meeting.

Directions

AMCO
BUILDING

International Foods plc
Wilkie plc
Park and Moss

Central Bank

You are here

AMCO

Spencer Street

Moorhouse Road

Post Office

1 Preview

*Somebody wants to go
to Park and Moss's office.*

Look at the map and give them directions.

2 Language Focus A

Read the fax and look at the maps. Then complete the fax with these expressions.

a) follow the signs   d) leave the motorway   f) on the left x 2
b) turn left   e) on the sixth floor   g) don't
c) go through

FACSIMILE

From   Stella Smith, Research Department,
        Johnson Matthey, Technology Centre

To   Gordon Kay, Pax Consultants, Oxford

Following our telephone conversation today, here are two maps showing the way to our Technology Centre. From Oxford take the M4 motorway going east. [1]..... at Junction 6 and [2]..... for Reading (B480 and B481). [3]..... Nettlebed. As you approach Sonning Common, there's a garage [4]..... . [5]..... go into the town; [6]..... at the garage. The Technology Centre is [7]..... . My office is [8]..... .

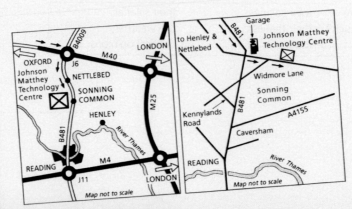

LANGUAGE SUMMARY A

Giving directions
Take the M40 motorway.
Leave the motorway at Junction 6.
Follow the signs for Reading.
Go through Nettlebed.
Don't go into the town.
Turn left at the garage.

Explaining location
There's a garage on the left.
My office is on the sixth floor.

3 Practice

Look again at the maps in the fax. Explain the way from London to the Technology Centre by road.

4 Numberwork

4.1 📟 Listen and number each floor when you hear it.

ground	☐	3rd	☐	14th	☐
1st	☐	4th	1	20th	☐
2nd	☐	13th	☐	22nd	☐

NUMBERWORK SUMMARY

When we talk about floors in a building we use ordinal numbers.

Cardinal numbers	Ordinal numbers
one	first (1st)
two	second (2nd)
three	third (3rd)
four	fourth (4th)
five	fifth (5th)
six	sixth (6th)
seven	seventh (7th)
fourteen	fourteenth (14th)
twenty	twentieth (20th)
twenty-one	twenty-first (21st)

CHECK!

When do we not add th to make an ordinal number?

4.2 Draw a plan of a building. Show which departments are on which floors.

4.3 Work with a partner. Take turns to describe your plan to your partner. Ask him or her to draw the plan.

Model

There are five floors. Reception and Sales are on the ground floor.

5 Wordwork

5.1 Match the words and the pictures.

1 go along   3 go into
2 go through   4 go out of

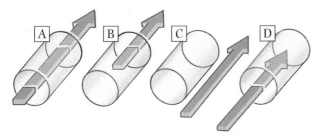

5.2 Which of these sentences are not correct?

1 a) Go along the street.
 b) Go along the town.
 c) Go along the building.
2 a) Don't go out of the building.
 b) Don't go out of the town.
 c) Don't go out of the motorway.
3 a) Go through the street.
 b) Go through the motorway.
 c) Go through the town centre.
4 a) Go into the building.
 b) Go into the street.
 c) Go into the motorway.

6 Language Focus B

6.1 📟 Listen to a conversation in an office in Paris. Mark the location of the taxi rank on the map.

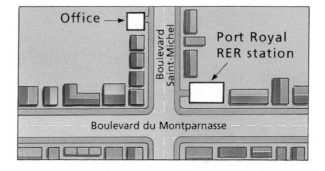

6.2 📟 Listen again. What are the missing words?

1 What two questions does the man ask?
 a) . . . . . a taxi rank near here?
 b) . . . . . get there, please?
2 The man checks the directions. What does he say?
 . . . . . Saint-Michel and Montparnasse.
3 The woman gives more information. What does she say?
 It's . . . . . the entrance to the Port Royal RER station.

LANGUAGE SUMMARY B

Questions
Is there a taxi rank near here?
Can you tell me how to get there, please?

Explaining location
It's on the corner of boulevard Saint-Michel and boulevard du Montparnasse.
It's opposite the entrance to the Port Royal RER station.
It's next to the bank.

7 Practice

You are at a restaurant in your town with a visitor. The visitor asks for directions.

Work with a partner. Give him or her directions. Take turns to be the host and the visitor. Talk about these points.

a bank   a taxi rank   a night club   a post office
a cinema

Model

A Is there a bank near here?

B Yes, there's one ....

A Can you tell me how to get there?

B Yes, of course. Go out of the restaurant and ....

8 Output

8.1 Draw a map showing the way to your office.

8.2 What words do you need to give directions to a visitor? Organise your words in wordfields.

8.3 Write a fax to a visitor giving directions to your office.

LEARNING TIP

- There are many different words you can use when giving directions. It is not necessary to know them all.
- It can be helpful to organise the words you need in wordfields like these.

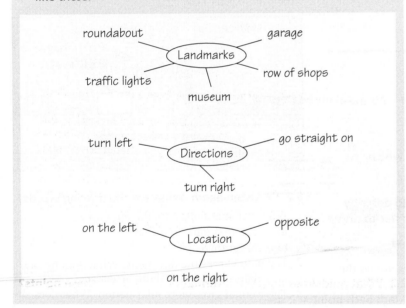

Guidelines

1 Preview

Look at these aircraft signs.
What do they mean?

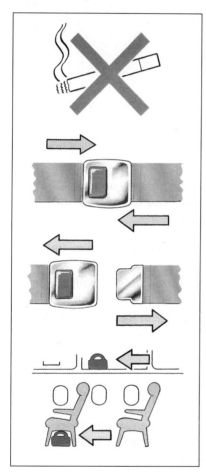

2 Language Focus

2.1 Read the information about air travel.

A Guide for Travellers
Customs and Excise Notice 1.

Travelling within the EU

When you travel directly to the UK from another EU country
- you don't have to go through UK Customs
- you should use the blue exit
- you mustn't bring prohibited goods (e.g. drugs, weapons) into the UK

Travelling from outside the EU

When you travel to the UK from a non-EU country
- you must go through UK Customs

Tips for Travellers

Air travel can be stressful! Try these tips from a regular traveller.

- Avoid checking in late. Remember that there can be problems on the journey to the airport, so you should leave home early.
- Make sure you wear comfortable clothes on long flights. You don't have to wear a business suit. If necessary, take it with you and change before you arrive.

**2.2 What guidelines does the information give about these points?
Mark each point 1, 2 or 3.**

1 = don't do this
2 = do this
3 = you can choose to do this or not

a) go through Customs if you travel from outside the EU ☐
b) go through Customs if you travel from within the EU ☐
c) use the blue exit if you travel from within the EU ☐
d) bring drugs into the UK ☐1
e) check in late ☐
f) leave home early ☐
g) wear comfortable clothes on long flights ☐
h) wear a business suit on a plane ☐

Telling people to do something
You **must go** through Customs.
Make sure you wear comfortable clothes.
You **should leave** home early.

Telling people not to do something
You **mustn't bring** drugs into the UK.
Avoid checking in late.

Telling people they can choose
You **don't have to wear** a business suit.

CHECK!

1 Put these words in the appropriate place on the line.

must   don't have to   make sure   mustn't
should   avoid

**100%
No** **100%
Yes**

2 Which form of the verb wear do you use after

	wear	wearing
a) must?	☐	☐
b) should?	☐	☐
c) mustn't?	☐	☐
d) don't have to?	☐	☐
e) avoid?	☐	☐

3 Practice

3.1 Look again at the Preview on page 47. What do the signs tell you? Use words from the Language Summary.

3.2 Give more guidelines for air travellers. Talk about these points.
Example: You should put your hand baggage in the overhead locker.

1 put your hand baggage in the overhead locker
2 read the safety instructions
3 smoke in the toilets
4 use the oxygen mask if there is an emergency
5 drink wine with your meal
6 call the flight attendant if you feel ill

3.3 Think about your organisation. What guidelines does it give to its employees? Complete the sentences.

1 Employees must . . . . . .
2 Employees mustn't . . . . . .
3 Employees don't have to . . . . . .
4 Employees should . . . . . .

3.4 Here are some more tips for stress-free travel. Say them in another way, using make sure you + verb or avoid verb + ing.

1 Don't book your flight at the last minute.
2 Take out travel insurance.
3 Don't take more than one piece of hand baggage.
4 Reconfirm your flight 72 hours before you fly.

4 Reading

4.1 Student A: Look at page 112.
Student B: Read the article about jet lag. What does it say about food, drink and exercise on long flights? Make notes.

How to avoid jet lag
● ● ● ● ● ● ● ● ● ● ● ● ● ●

TIPS FOR REGULAR TRAVELLERS

Travellers can reduce the effects of jet lag by changing their eating and drinking patterns. If you want to sleep on a plane, you should eat foods such as bread, pasta or cakes. Avoid eating high-protein foods such as meat, eggs or cheese. Don't drink tea or coffee for two days before flying. Remember that you don't have to eat and drink everything that they offer you on a plane. You should avoid alcohol and drink at least two litres of water on a six-hour flight. Exercise also helps. You can do simple exercises in your seat, or walk around the plane. ∎

4.2 Work with a partner. Tell him or her about the tips in your article.

4.3 What does your partner's article say about jet lag? Make notes about time and sleep.

5 Listening

An Indian, Mr Singh, is talking to a German couple, Mr and Mrs Meyer.

5.1 ⌨ Listen to their conversation and answer the question.

Are the Meyers going to India
a) on holiday?
b) on a business trip?
c) to work and live there?

5.2 ⌨ Listen again. What does Mr Singh say about

1 dealing with Indian employees?
2 dealing with Indian colleagues?
3 guidelines for women?
4 travelling in India?

6 Output

6.1 Prepare guidelines for a foreigner coming to work in your country. Think about these points.

dealing with employees or management
dealing with colleagues
travelling
any other important points

6.2 Present your guidelines.

Telephone Calls

1 Preview

Answer these questions.

1 When you answer the phone at work, what do you say?
2 When you ask for somebody on the phone, what do you say?
3 What do you do and say if somebody speaks too fast on the telephone?

2 Language Focus

2.1 🖭 Listen to two telephone calls. Match the sentences and the speakers.

1 How's the weather in England?
2 How can I help you?
3 Park and Moss, good afternoon.
4 Just a moment, please.
5 Hello, Tax Department.

2.2 What are the missing words?

Conversation 1

CHRISTINE SAVILLE   Tax Department.
WOLFGANG BINDER   Good morning. .... Wolfgang Binder. .... Christine Saville?
CHRISTINE SAVILLE   Yes, ... How are you, Wolfgang?
WOLFGANG BINDER   Fine, thanks. How's the weather in England?
CHRISTINE SAVILLE   It's wonderful. Very hot. So, ... you, Wolfgang?
WOLFGANG BINDER   Well, ... your visit next week.

Conversation 2

RECEPTIONIST   Park and Moss, good afternoon.
ALEC MACFARLANE   Good afternoon. .... to .... Christine Saville, please.
RECEPTIONIST   Just a moment, please.
CHRISTINE SAVILLE   Hello, Tax Department.
ALEC MACFARLANE   Hello. .... Alec Macfarlane ..... Wilcox International.
CHRISTINE SAVILLE   Oh, hello Alec. What can I do for you?
ALEC MACFARLANE   .... some information ..... tax guidelines in Germany.

2.3 🖭 Listen again. Are your words the same as the words on the cassette?

Christine Saville

Wolfgang Binder

Receptionist

Christine Saville

Alec Macfarlane

LANGUAGE SUMMARY

The person who answers the phone says

Park and Moss, good morning.

Hello, Tax Department.

How can I help you?

What can I do for you?

The caller says

This is | Wolfgang Binder.
| Alec Macfarlane from Wilcox International.

Is that Christine Saville?

I'd like to speak to Christine Saville, please.

I'm calling about...

I'd like some information about...

CHECK!

The expressions in this conversation are not appropriate on the phone. How can you change them?

A Are you John Smith?

B Yes, I am.

A Here is Pat Black at ABC.

B What do you want?

3 Practice

Work with a partner and have telephone conversations. Use the role cards your teacher gives you.

4 Culture Focus

4.1 Answer these questions about your country.

1 When you call an office and ask to speak to a person, do you use that person's
   a) family name only?
   b) first and family names?
   c) title and family name?

2 When you make a business call to somebody you know, do you
   a) begin with a business question?
   b) ask **How are you?**
   c) ask about the weather?
   d) ask other questions?

3 Is small talk on the phone
   a) appropriate during a business call?
   b) not very useful?

4.2 Answer the same questions about another country you know well.

CULTURE SUMMARY

Asking to speak to somebody on the phone

When you make a business call to an English-speaking country, you should use the first name and family name of the person you want to speak to, or his/her title (Mr, Mrs, Ms etc.) and family name.

Starting a phone conversation with people you know

Many English-speaking people ask general questions, for example about the weather, when they call people they know. It is a good idea to do this when you make a call to an English-speaking business contact.

5 Tactics Focus

5.1 🔲 Listen to two versions of a telephone call to the British Airways office in Athens. Answer these questions.

1 What is the reason for the call?
2 Does the caller explain what he wants clearly?
3 In which version does the British Airways assistant keep more control of the call?

5.2 How does the assistant ask the caller to

1 speak more slowly?
2 tell her his flight number?
3 repeat the dates?
4 repeat his name?
5 spell his name?

TACTICS SUMMARY

When you make or receive a call, keep control of the conversation.

■ Ask the other person to slow down.
  Could you speak more slowly, please?

■ Ask the other person to repeat key facts.
  Could you repeat the dates, please?
  Can I have your name again, please?

■ Ask for information in the order you need it.
  Can I have your flight number first, please?

■ Ask the other person to spell names or addresses.
  Could you spell that, please?

■ Make a check-list of points you want to ask before you make your call.

6 Speechwork

Here are the letters of the English alphabet.

A   B   C   D   E   F   G   H   I   J
K   L   M   N   O   P   Q   R   S   T
U   V   W   X   Y   Z

6.1 Which letters have the same sound? Complete the table.

B (x 7)
F (x 6)
A (x 3)
Q (x 2)

6.2 Which letters are left?

6.3 ▣ Listen and check your answers.

6.4 Choose three names which you think are difficult to spell. Spell them to your partner. He/she must write them down.

7 Practice

7.1 Work with a partner and have conversations.
Model
A Good morning.
B Good morning. I'd like some information about your organisation.
A Would you like a copy of our brochure?
B Yes, please. My name's . . . . . and I work for . . . .
A Can I have your name again, please?
B Yes, it's . . . . . .
A And your company name?
B It's . . . . . .
A Could you spell that, please?
B . . . . . .
A What's your address?
B . . . . . .
A Could you speak more slowly, please?

7.2 Work with a partner.
Student A: Look at page 112.
Student B: You are on business in Jakarta. You have a ticket for flight GA762 to Seoul tomorrow at 16.30, but you want to fly the day after tomorrow. Phone Garuda Indonesian Airways and try to change your flight.

7.3 You work for Alitalia in Milan. A passenger calls you. Find out

1 the passenger's name.
2 the flight number.
3 the destination.
4 the date booked.
5 the date he/she wants to fly.

8 Output

8.1 Think of four questions to ask a partner about his or her organisation or department (e.g. location, number of employees).

8.2 Work with a partner and have two telephone conversations. Take turns to be A and B.

Roles	You choose.
Relationship	You choose.
Place	On the telephone.

Conversation Plan
A Phone B. Say who you are.
B Answer the phone. Find out what A wants.
A Explain the reason for your call. Ask your questions.
B Answer A's questions.
A Ask B to repeat or spell things, if necessary. Write the answers to your questions.

16

Offers and Requests

1 Preview

What do you do and say in these situations?

1 A client calls your office and asks to speak to one of your colleagues. Your colleague isn't in the office.

2 Your colleague is late for a meeting with a client. The client is in your colleague's office.

3 Your colleague arranged to take a visitor to lunch. Now he tells you he can't do it.

4 You call to speak to a supplier. She isn't there.

5 You are abroad on business. You need to change your flight, but you have meetings all day.

2 Language Focus

2.1 Look at the pictures. Complete the conversations with these sentences.

a) Would you like to look at our new brochure?

b) Could you call us a taxi?

c) Could you give him a message?

d) Would you like to speak to his assistant, Emma Jones?

e) I'll pick them up on my way to work.

f) Would you like a coffee?

2.2 Find four examples of offers. Which words introduce the offers?

2.3 Find two examples of requests. Which words introduce the requests?

I'm sorry, Mr Nakatane isn't in the office this morning. .....

No, it's OK, thank you. I'll call this afternoon.

1 A call to Mr Nakatane's office at Interbank in London

I'm sorry, he's in a meeting.

Yes, of course.

I see. .....

2 Another call to Mr Nakatane's office

I'm afraid Mr Nakatane is still in a meeting. .....

No, thanks. I'm fine.

3 In Emma Jones' office

Yes, please.

I offered to meet Mr Konus and Mrs Suskova at the airport tomorrow, but I don't think I can do it now.

Don't worry. .....

4 In Mr Nakatane's office

We're a little late for our next meeting. .....

Yes, of course.

5 At the end of the meeting

LANGUAGE SUMMARY

Requests

QUESTIONS		ANSWERS
Could you	call us a taxi?	Yes, certainly.
	give him a message?	Yes, of course.

Offers

QUESTIONS		ANSWERS
Would you like to	speak to Emma Jones?	Yes, please.
	look at the brochure?	No, it's OK, thank you.
I'll	pick you up on the way to work.	
	call you a taxi.	

Pronouns
me/you/him/her/us/them

3 Practice

3.1 Read this fax from Emma Jones to the Central Bank of Slovakia. Complete it with her, him, me, us and you.

FAX

To Karol Konus

Re: Our visit to Bratislava

We now have flights to Vienna on Friday 4 June, arriving 10.00. Could you meet [1]..... at Vienna airport?

Mr Nakatane has a return flight on 4 June at 19.30, but I would like to stay for the weekend. Could you book [2]..... a hotel in Bratislava?

Mr Nakatane needs to talk to Irena Suskova about the arrangements for the meeting on Friday. Could you ask [3]..... to call [4]..... later today?

I found an interesting article about the Central Bank in The Economist. I'll bring [5]..... a copy.

3.2 Look at the picture and answer these questions.

1 What can the assistant offer?
2 What can the boss ask his assistant to do?

3.3 Look at the picture and answer the question.

What can the assistant offer?

4 Numberwork

4.1 🖭 Listen. Which four numbers do you hear?

301 756759
203 765759
301 976755
302 757595
230 977565
301 755796
302 765579

NUMBERWORK SUMMARY

```
international  city code    extension
   code
   00  1   302  975765,  ext  5224
   └─┬─┘         └──┬──┘
 country code    number
```

Say each figure separately
975765 nine-seven-five-seven-six-
five
Say 0 as oh or zero
302 three-oh-two
three-zero-two
When two numbers are the same and are together, you can say double or you can say the figures separately
5224 five-double two-four
five-two-two-four

4.2 How do you say these telephone numbers?

1 30 81 1579947
2 1 212 308 6445
3 44 171 873 3006
4 6145 160066

4.3 Work with a partner. Ask for his or her office phone number.

5 Conversation Focus

5.1 Read the conversation. The underlined parts are not appropriate for the situation. How can you change them?

RICHARD CARTER I want to speak to Andy Mitchell. Is he in the office?
RECEPTIONIST No, I'm sorry he's not here today.
RICHARD CARTER Oh, no. This is Richard Carter. I need to speak to him.
RECEPTIONIST Do you want his home number?
RICHARD CARTER No. Just tell him I called. Ask him to ring me tomorrow morning. The number is 091 56844.
RECEPTIONIST OK.

5.2 🖭 Now listen to the real conversation. What do they say?

CONVERSATION SUMMARY

If you want to sound polite on the telephone
Would you like...? sounds more polite than **Do you want...?**
Could you tell him I called? sounds more polite than **Tell him I called.**
The way you say the words is also important.

6 Speechwork

6.1 🖭 Listen to three questions. You hear each question twice. Which sounds more polite, 1 or 2?

	1	2
1 Would you like his home number?	✔	☐
2 Could you tell him I called?	☐	☐
3 Could you ask him to ring me?	☐	☐

6.2 🖭 Listen to two requests and answers. You hear each answer twice. Which sounds more polite, 1 or 2?

	1	2
1 A Could you tell him I called? B Yes, of course.	☐	☐
2 A Could you ask him to ring me? B Yes, certainly.	☐	☐

7 Practice

Look again at the Preview on page 53. Work with a partner and have a conversation for each situation.

8 Output

8.1 Find out the name of one of your partner's colleagues.

8.2 Work with a partner and have conversations. Use the role cards your teacher gives you.

A Top Firm

1 Wordwork

Complete this list.

Simple present	Simple past
begin(s)	1 . . . . .
2	went up
is/are	3 . . . . .
4	opened
rise(s)	5 . . . . .
6	sold
set(s) up	7 . . . . .
8	started
work(s)	9 . . . . .

2 Writing

Look at the time line and complete the article about Ecco, a Danish shoe company.

Date	Event
1928	Karl Toosbuy born near Copenhagen
1944–48	learns to make shoes
1963	sets up Ecco in south of Denmark
1968	Ecco is the main shoe manufacturer in Denmark
1977	sales rise to over Dkr1 million
1984	Ecco opens its first foreign factory in Portugal
1991	Ecco opens a factory in Indonesia
1992	sales go up to over Dkr1,000 million
1993	production starts in China under licence
1994	production begins in Ecco's factory in Thailand

Karl Toosbuy

Karl Toosbuy [1] . . . . . Ecco in 1963. Five years later, it [2] . . . . . the main shoe manufacturer in Denmark and in 1977 sales [3] . . . . . to over Dkr1 million. The company's first foreign factory [4] . . . . . in Portugal in 1984.

In the 1990s, the company continued to expand. Ecco [5] . . . . . another factory in Indonesia in 1991. The company's sales [6] . . . . . to over Dkr1,000 million the following year. In 1993 they [7] . . . . . to produce shoes under licence in China and the year after that production [8] . . . . . in a new Ecco factory in Thailand.

The company now [9] . . . . . more than seven million pairs of shoes per year all over the world. The main markets are Germany, Japan and Denmark.

Today Ecco is a big international company, but it is still a family business – Karl Toosbuy's wife and daughter [10] . . . . . there in the past and now his son-in-law is the Development Director.

3 Speaking

Work with a partner.
Student A: Look at page 113.
Student B: You received this fax from the Publicity Department at Chupa Chups, a Spanish confectionery company. The fax is not clear. Phone your partner in the Publicity Department and check the information. Correct the parts that are not clear.

page 2

When his father retired in 1957, Enrique Bernat took over Chupa Chups. At that time the company had more than ⟨ ⟩ products. He decided to concentrate on only one product – lollipops. This policy was very successful and sales in Spain ⟨...⟩ in the 1960s.

The company began to export its lollipops at the end of the 1960s. Chupa Chups opened its first foreign factory in ⟨...⟩ in 1969. In ⟨...⟩ production began at a factory in St Petersburg to supply the Russian market. The United States and Japan are other big markets.

The early 1990s were difficult years for many companies, but Chupa Chups' sales ⟨...⟩ by nearly 8 per cent in 1992.

Like many Spanish companies, Chupa Chups is a family business. Enrique Bernat's three sons and one of his daughters work for the company, and his wife is Chupa Chups' ⟨...⟩ Manager.

4 Listening

▣ Listen to an interview with Ingmar Borg, an employee in the Publicity Department of Ikea, a Swedish furniture company. Complete the table.

Started by	Ingvar Kamprad
Date	1
First store	
place	south of Sweden
date	2
First store outside Scandinavia	
place	3
date	4
Factories	
numbers	5
Stores now	
number	6
places	in 24 countries
Main market	7
Other markets	8
Family in company	9

5 Practice

These guidelines are for a competition to find Europe's Top Family Firm.

Explain the guidelines.

Example: It must be a European company.

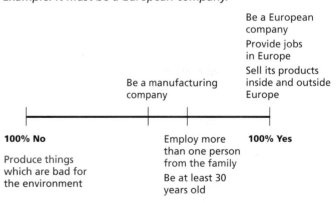

6 Output

Which company should win the competition – Ecco, Chupa Chups or Ikea? Why?

Plans

1 Preview

Talk about your company's or department's plans for the next twelve months.

2 Language Focus

Keatings are planning a quality control seminar. Patrick Mulligan, Head Buyer at Keatings, wrote some notes on the provisional programme below.

2.1 What does Patrick Mulligan want to know about?

KEATINGS

Keatings Quality Control Seminar

LOCATION Park Hotel, Kilkenny
DATES   Monday 9 March to
          Wednesday 11 March

Provisional Programme
                                    Transport to Kilkenny
                                    – coach?
Sunday 8 March
    Delegates arrive at Dublin airport
    ───────────────── Evening programme?
Monday 9 March
    Opening speech ── Who?
    Presentation: Quality Control Systems
    in Keatings
    Lunch
    Workshop: Distribution problems
    Reception ── Where?

                        Which supplier?
Tuesday 10 March   /
    Visit to local supplier (to be confirmed)
    Lunch ──────── at the hotel?
    Reports on visit
    Workshop: Food management
    Dinner and pub visit

Wednesday 11 March
    Visit to Keatings' Dublin warehouse
    Transfer to airport 12.30 p.m.

2.2 📼 Listen to a conversation between Patrick Mulligan, Helen Brown, a buyer, and her assistant, Jonathan Fox. What are the answers to Patrick's questions?

2.3 📼 Listen again. What do Helen and Jonathan say about the plans? Complete these sentences.

1 There's no special programme because the coach ..... at the hotel until about 9.30 p.m.
2 ..... the presentation on quality control at the end of the morning.
3 ..... also ..... to invite the mayor of Kilkenny, but we're not sure if he can come.
4 ..... John McCormack tomorrow to discuss the visit.
5 Maurizio Rivella ..... until Tuesday morning.

2.4 Match words from A and B to make Patrick Mulligan's questions.

Example: 1 = c

A	B
1 What	a) are we having the reception?
2 Who's	b) are you planning to visit?
3 Where	c) are the delegates doing on
4 Which supplier	Sunday evening?
5 Are	d) giving the opening speech?
6 Is	e) Maurizio Rivella coming?
	f) they having lunch at the hotel?

2.5 📼 Listen again. Are your questions the same as the questions on the cassette?

LANGUAGE SUMMARY

Asking about plans

Are they **having** lunch at the hotel on Tuesday?

Is Maurizio Rivella **coming**?

What **are** the delegates **doing** on Sunday evening?

Who**'s giving** the opening speech?

Where **are** we **having** the reception?

Which supplier **are** you **planning** to visit?

Explaining plans

You**'re giving** the presentation on quality control.

I**'m seeing** John McCormack tomorrow.

Maurizio Rivella **isn't arriving** until Tuesday morning.

We**'re planning** to invite the mayor of Kilkenny.

CHECK!

1 **Does Maurizio Rivella isn't arriving until Tuesday morning** mean he is coming
   a) before Tuesday morning?
   b) on Tuesday morning?
2 **Make sentences.**
   a) I/fly/to Paris/on Monday.
   b) Who/you/plan/to visit there?
   c) I/not/come back/until Sunday.

3 Speechwork

🔲 Listen to nine sentences about plans. After you hear each sentence, repeat what you hear. Then write the full sentence.

4 Practice

Look at 2.1 again. Explain the programme for the Keatings seminar.

5 Wordwork

Complete the diary with these time expressions.

1 tomorrow
2 next Thursday afternoon
3 on Sunday night
4 the day after tomorrow
5 this weekend
6 on Thursday morning
7 next Tuesday
8 this Friday evening
9 tonight
10 tomorrow evening

6 Practice

6.1 Complete this note with prepositions if you think they are necessary.

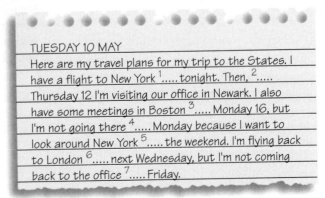

TUESDAY 10 MAY

Here are my travel plans for my trip to the States. I have a flight to New York [1]..... tonight. Then, [2]..... Thursday 12 I'm visiting our office in Newark. I also have some meetings in Boston [3]..... Monday 16, but I'm not going there [4]..... Monday because I want to look around New York [5]..... the weekend. I'm flying back to London [6]..... next Wednesday, but I'm not coming back to the office [7]..... Friday.

6.2 Write the note again. Use dates to make it clear.

6.3 Think about the next two weeks. What are your plans? Make notes like this.

Plans I'm sure about	
Date/Day	Plan
Friday	go to Paris on business

Provisional plans	
Date/Day	Plan
Weekend	spend it there

6.4 Work with a partner. Ask and answer questions about your plans for the next two weeks.

Models

A What are you doing on Friday?

B I'm going to Paris on business.

A What about the weekend?

B I'm planning to spend the weekend there.

7 Output

Some foreign visitors are visiting your organisation next month.

7.1 Work in groups. Decide on some details about the visit (e.g. how many people and what their interests are).

7.2 Plan a programme for the visit.

7.3 Present your programme.

LEARNING TIP

When a foreigner speaks to you in your language, what is important to you? Number these points from 1 to 6 (1 = very important, 6 = not very important).

1 he/she almost never makes grammar mistakes ☐

2 he/she sounds friendly and polite ☐

3 he/she has a very good accent ☐

4 he/she knows a lot of words ☐

5 he/she speaks fluently ☐

6 other points (what?) ☐

When you speak to a foreigner in English, what is important to you about your English? Is the order of points the same?

▭ **Look at the cartoon and listen to the cassette. What is the speaker's problem?**

Then on Tuesday we are taking you to visit our new factory. It is very modern and very interesting.

■ In class

When you **start** to practise new language points, try to be correct and careful. Don't worry if you don't speak fluently. At other times, try to speak as fluently as you can. Don't worry if you make some mistakes.

■ Outside class

When you speak to business contacts in English, they don't usually worry if you make some mistakes. But it is important to sound friendly and polite and to speak as fluently as you can.

Appointments

1 Preview

1.1 Answer these questions about meetings in your country.

1 You want a business meeting with a client. Do you arrange it
   a) about two or three weeks before?
   b) about two or three days before?
   c) on the day you want the meeting?
2 You have an appointment at 10.30. Do you arrive
   a) about 15 minutes before?
   b) at exactly 10.30?
   c) between 10.30 and 11.00?
3 You arrive for a meeting on time, but the other person is not there. Do you feel angry after
   a) about 10 minutes?
   b) about 30 minutes?
   c) an hour or more?

1.2 Answer the same questions about another country you know well.

2 Language Focus

Lana Russell works for the Glasgow office of Interconsult. It helps companies to do business in other countries.

2.1 Read this fax for Lana Russell.

FAX

From   Akira Miyazawa
To   Lana Russell

Thank you for the information you sent about suppliers near Glasgow. Mr Noguchi and I are coming to the UK next month. We're planning to be in Glasgow from 7–9 September and would like to meet representatives from these companies:

1 Scot-Tech
2 Clyde Electric
3 SETAL

Could you arrange meetings for us?

Lana Russell telephones Charles Cameron of Scot-Tech.

2.2 📼 Listen to their conversation and note the day, date and time of the meeting.

2.3 What are the missing words?

CHARLES CAMERON	I'll get my diary. Oh, Tuesday's . . . . I'm visiting clients in Birmingham all day.
LANA RUSSELL	OK. . . . . Wednesday?
CHARLES CAMERON	Wednesday's . . . . . , but the morning's a bit . . . . . .
LANA RUSSELL	. . . . the afternoon then?
CHARLES CAMERON	Yes, ...
LANA RUSSELL	What time?
CHARLES CAMERON	Let me see. . . . . . 2.30 . . . . . ?
LANA RUSSELL	Yes, I think . . . .

2.4 📼 Listen again. Are your words the same as the words on the cassette?

LANGUAGE SUMMARY

Suggesting dates and times

QUESTIONS			ANSWERS
What	about	Wednesday?	Yes, that's fine.
How		the afternoon?	No, that's not possible.
Is	2.30 Tuesday	OK?	

Explaining a problem
Tuesday's not possible. I'm visiting clients in Birmingham all day.
The morning's a bit difficult.

Agreeing

The afternoon's	fine.
Tuesday's	OK.

3 Practice

3.1 Work with a partner and arrange a meeting.

Model

A Can we meet next week to discuss ..... ?

B Which day?

A How about ..... ?

B ..... not possible. ....

A OK. What about ..... then?

B Yes, that's fine, but the morning's a bit difficult.

A What about the ..... then?

B That's OK.

A What time?

B Is ..... OK?

A Yes, that's fine.

3.2 Practise suggesting dates and times for meetings next week.

Conversation Plan 1

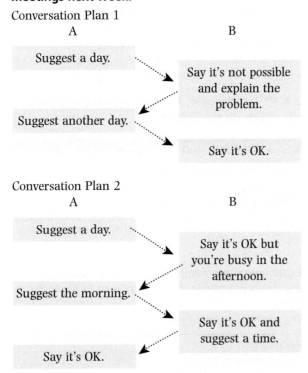

Conversation Plan 2

4 Numberwork

4.1 What are the dates of public holidays (e.g. Christmas, Independence Day, National Day) in your country?

NUMBERWORK SUMMARY

You see	You say
UK ENGLISH	
7 September (7/9)	the seventh of September
	September the seventh
22 May (22/5)	the twenty-second of May
	May the twenty-second
US ENGLISH	
September 7 (9/7)	September seventh
May 22 (5/22)	May twenty-second

4.2 When are these meetings? How do you say the dates in different ways?

1 11.30 Friday 21/10   4 16.45 31/7 Wednesday
2 Thursday 1/4 10.00   5 Monday 12/2 3.20
3 Tuesday 3/12 2.15

5 Tactics Focus

Lana Russell telephones Ian Campbell of Clyde Electric. After the telephone call she sends a fax to Mr Miyazawa.

5.1 🖭 Listen to Lana's conversation with Ian Campbell. Are the date and the time in her fax correct?

> Mr Campbell of Clyde Electric can meet you on Tuesday 9 September at ten o'clock. Please contact me if there is a problem.

5.2 Read these sentences. They can help Lana to avoid the mistakes she made with the dates and times.

a) 11 o'clock.

b) So Thursday morning.

c) So, that's 11 o'clock on Thursday 9 September.

d) So Tuesday and Wednesday aren't possible.

5.3 Complete this extract from Lana's conversation with Ian Campbell with the sentences from 5.2.

IAN CAMPBELL   Let me see. Well, Tuesday's not possible. I'm at a seminar until Wednesday lunchtime.

LANA RUSSELL   Are you coming back to the office in the afternoon?

IAN CAMPBELL   No, the seminar is in London and I'm driving back to Glasgow.

LANA RUSSELL   ¹..... How about Thursday then?

IAN CAMPBELL   Yes, that's fine but I prefer the morning.

LANA RUSSELL   OK. ²..... Is 10 o'clock OK?

IAN CAMPBELL   Actually, it's a bit early. Can we say 11 o'clock?

LANA RUSSELL   ³..... OK. ⁴..... I'll send a fax to Japan and call you again to confirm.

5.4 🔲 Listen. Is your conversation the same as the conversation on the cassette?

TACTICS SUMMARY

When you arrange a meeting on the telephone

- Repeat dates and times.
  So Tuesday and Wednesday aren't possible.
  So Thursday morning at 11 o'clock.
- At the end of the call repeat all the details of the meeting.
  So that's 11 o'clock on Thursday 9 September at your office.

---

6 Practice

6.1 Work with a partner. Have a conversation like the one in 3.1. Make sure you repeat days, dates and times.

6.2 Work with a partner and have a telephone conversation. Use the role cards your teacher gives you.

7 Output

7.1 Write six appointments in your diary for next week.

7.2 Work with a partner and have a telephone conversation.

Roles	One person is the caller, the other answers the phone.
Relationship	You choose.
Place	On the telephone.
Task	Arrange a meeting for next week. You choose the reason for the meeting.

19

Products

1 Preview

What do these customers look for when they buy a coffee machine?

a housewife
the manager of a coffee bar
the manager of a company canteen

2 Language Focus

Complete the text with these words.

a) is not designed for
b) is available in
c) for making
d) uses

e) are designed for
f) are available in
g) can
h) takes

Café Express

Italian coffee machines

Café Express produce a range of machines ¹..... coffee and other hot drinks. Our machines ²..... commercial use, either for self–service or for waiter operation. All our machines are practical, well designed and easy to use. They ³..... various models for different uses.

The EX-11 ⁴..... fresh coffee and ⁵..... make espresso or cappuccino. It ⁶..... 11 seconds to make a cup of espresso and one minute to make a cappuccino. It ⁷..... self–service use. It ⁸..... four different sizes.

Describing the function of a product
We produce machines for making coffee.

They are It is not	designed for	commercial use. self-service use.

Describing the features of a product

They are It is	available in	various models. four sizes. two colours.

It can make espresso or cappuccino.
It uses fresh coffee.
It takes 11 seconds to make an espresso.

CHECK!

1 **Which form of the verb do you use after for?**
2 **Put the verbs in the correct form.**
    a) A fax is for ..... (send) letters.
    b) Photocopiers are for ..... (copy) documents.

3 Practice

The Concept 2000 is another coffee machine from Café Express.

Use this information to describe it.

instant products
Italian-style espresso, cappuccino and hot chocolate
3 seconds – espresso
10 seconds – cappuccino or hot chocolate
self-service or waiter operation
this size only

4 Numberwork

A customer telephones a salesman at Café Express to ask about the size of the Concept 2000.

4.1 🖭 Listen to their conversation. What are the dimensions?

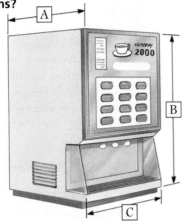

4.2 🖭 Listen again and complete these questions.

1 What's the . . . . . of it?
2 And what's the . . . . . of it?
3 And . . . . is it?

4.3 Complete these sentences.

1 The Concept 2000 is 435mm . . . . . .
2 The . . . . . of it is 740mm.
3 It's 505mm . . . . . .

NUMBERWORK SUMMARY

The	height depth width	is	740mm. 505mm. 435mm.	It's	740mm 505mm 435mm	high. deep. wide.

4.4 Work with a partner.
Student A: Look at page 113.
Student B: Answer your partner's questions about the EX-11A and EX-11B coffee makers.

	Height	Depth	Width	Cost
EX-11A	485mm	580mm	580mm	$2,500
EX-11B	485mm	580mm	740mm	$3,000
EX-11C				
EX-11D				

4.5 Now ask your partner about the EX-11C and EX-11D and complete the table.

5 Wordwork

5.1 Match the adjectives with the nouns they can describe.

Adjectives	Nouns
1 good	a) cost
2 efficient	b) machine
3 bad	c) quality
4 high	d) service
5 low	
6 fast	
7 slow	
8 quick	
9 practical	

5.2 Which of these sentences have adjectives in them? Which have adverbs?

1 Our machines are easy to use.
2 Waiters learn to use them easily.
3 With our machines you can serve your customers efficiently.
4 The Concept 2000 is a very efficient machine.

CHECK!

How do you usually make an adverb from an adjective?

5.3 Complete the list.

Adjectives	Adverbs
quick	quickly
easy	1 . . . . .
2	slowly
efficient	3 . . . . .
4	well
bad	5 . . . . .
6	fast

5.4 Complete this advertisement. Use adjectives or adverbs from 5.1 and 5.3.

Concept 2000

[1]. . . . . quality at [2]. . . . . cost!

The Concept 2000 is a [3]. . . . . new machine for producing espresso, cappuccino and hot chocolate. It uses instant products, so you can make hot drinks [4]. . . . . and [5]. . . . . , and you can clean the machine [6]. . . . . .

Price: $2,250 including installation

6 Listening

Bob Temple is the owner of a coffee bar in Seattle. He telephones Renzo Fabbri, the Sales Manager of Café Express in the United States.

📟 **Listen to their conversation and answer the questions.**

1 Which machine do you think Renzo is planning to recommend, the EX-11 or the Concept 2000?
2 Why? Think about the function of the machine and the features that are important to Bob.

7 Writing

7.1 Read the letter Renzo sent to Bob after their phone call. Complete it with information about the machine you chose.

Dear Mr Temple,

Following our telephone call this morning, I enclose a brochure on our ¹..... coffee machine. I think this suits your needs.

We can supply the ²..... at a price of ³...... This includes installation and staff training.

If you need more information, please call me again.

Sincerely yours,

Renzo Fabbri

Renzo Fabbri
Sales Manager

7.2 Which expressions in the letter show that

1 Bob doesn't have to pay extra for installation and staff training?
2 there is a brochure in the envelope?
3 Bob and Renzo spoke on the phone?

7.3 Read this message to Renzo from his secretary.

Telephone Message

From Sue
To Renzo

I got a call from Mrs Coleman at Wilcox International. They want a hot drinks machine for their self-service canteen. She's the Catering Manager. The address is 156 Ocean Avenue, San Francisco.

7.4 Write a letter from Renzo to this customer. Use his letter to Bob Temple in 7.1 as a model.

8 Output

8.1 Choose a product your company makes or a product you use. Think about these questions.

1 What is the function of this product?
2 Is it designed for commercial use or home use?
3 Is it available in different models, sizes or colours?
4 What are the special features of this product? (e.g. is it slow, fast, efficient, practical, high quality?)

8.2 Describe your product. Do not say exactly what the product is. Other students must guess what it is from your description.

20

Invitations

1 Preview

How can you improve these conversations?

2 Language Focus

2.1 📟 Listen to three invitations and complete the table.

2.2 📟 Listen again and answer these questions.

1 What expressions do Bob, Christine and Ian use to invite people?
2 What expressions do Wolfgang and Lana use to accept their invitations?
3 What expression does Renzo use to decline his invitation?

LANGUAGE SUMMARY

Inviting

Would you like to	have dinner at my house tomorrow?
	go out for a meal later on?
	meet for lunch one day next week?

Accepting
Thank you very much. That's a good idea.
That would be very nice.

Declining
Thank you, but I'm flying back to San Francisco this evening.

CHECK!

Look again at the cartoons in the Preview. What should the people say?

3 Practice

Work with a partner and have conversations.

Conversation Plan
A Invite B (activity and day/time).
B Accept or decline.

	Bob Temple and Renzo Fabbri	Christine Saville and Wolfgang Binder	Ian Campbell and Lana Russell
What activity is the invitation for?			
What time/day is the invitation for?			
Does the person invited accept (say yes) or decline (say no)?			

4 Wordwork

Different expressions can describe a range of feelings about activities.

—   +   ++

4.1 What feelings do the underlined expressions in these sentences describe?

Example: 1 = +

1 I <u>like</u> classical music.
2 I'm <u>not very keen</u> on jazz.
3 I <u>really like</u> Italian films.
4 I <u>don't like</u> opera <u>very much</u>.

4.2 ▣ Listen and underline the stressed syllables in the sentences in 4.1.

Example: I <u>like</u> <u>clas</u>sical <u>mu</u>sic.

4.3 Choose three things you like from this list. Find other people in the class who like them too.

TV
computer games
rock music
tennis
football
foreign films
jazz
modern art

5 Conversation Focus

5.1 Look at the cartoons. The invitations are not successful. What should the woman do differently?

Would you like to come to a concert tonight?

No, I'm busy this evening.

Would you like to come to a concert tonight?

What kind of concert?

A modern jazz concert.

I'm not very keen on modern jazz.

Emma Jones of Interbank in London is on a business trip to Bratislava. She meets Irena Suskova of the Central Bank of Slovakia.

5.2 ▣ Listen to their conversation and answer these questions.

1 What is Irena's first question?
2 Irena invites Emma. What does she say?
3 Does Emma accept or decline?
4 What is Irena's next question?

5.3 Finish the conversation if Emma answers **yes**.

5.4 Finish the conversation if Emma answers **no**.

5.5 ▣ Now listen to two different versions of the end of this conversation. What does Irena say in each version?

CONVERSATION SUMMARY

When you invite people

■ Check first if the other person is free.
Do you have any plans for Saturday?
Are you doing anything on Saturday?
■ Then check what the other person likes.
Do you like opera?
■ If the answer is **yes**, invite him or her.
Tosca is on at the opera house here. Would you like to go to that?
■ If the answer is **no**, change your invitation.
Would you like to go out for dinner then?

6 Practice

6.1 What questions can you ask a visitor in these situations?

She's staying two more nights. I'm free tomorrow evening. There's a very good Indian restaurant near her hotel.

He isn't leaving until Friday, I think. I have an extra ticket for a jazz concert on Thursday night.

6.2 Work with a partner and have conversations. Use the role cards your teacher gives you.

7 Culture Focus

7.1 Answer these questions about your country with usually, sometimes or never.

1 A business contact visits you and is free in the evening. Do you
   a) invite him or her to dinner at your house?
   b) invite him or her to dinner in a restaurant?
2 An important client is in your town over the weekend. Do you
   a) invite him or her to spend the weekend with you and your family?
   b) invite him or her to go sightseeing?
3 A colleague or friend invites you to dinner at his or her house at 7.30 p.m. Do you
   a) arrive about 10 minutes early?
   b) arrive at exactly 7.30?
   c) arrive about 10 minutes late?
   d) arrive up to half an hour late?

7.2 Now answer the same questions about another country you know well.

CULTURE SUMMARY

Visits to people's homes

In some countries, for example the United States, people often invite visitors to their homes for dinner or to spend weekends with their family. In many other countries people don't usually do this.

Time

In countries where people invite visitors to their homes, customs about time can be very different. For example, in Sweden you should arrive at exactly the time your host suggested. In the UK it is polite to arrive about 10 minutes late for a dinner invitation at somebody's house.

8 Output

8.1 Think about these questions.

1 What activities are on in your town at the moment?
2 When are you free over the next three days?

8.2 Work with a partner and have conversations.

Roles	One of you is in the other's town for the next three days. Take turns to be the host and the visitor.
Relationship	You choose.
Task	Invite the visitor check when he/she is free. find out if he/she likes the activities you chose in 8.1. invite him/her.

Comparing Products and Services

1 Preview

What is special about these four types of communication?

the telephone   letters   faxes   e-mail

Which do you prefer for

business communication?
personal communication with friends or family?

2 Wordwork

2.1 Complete this extract from a brochure about a parcel service. Use these words.

collection   weight limit   delivery   insurance cover

Features of our service

Interpack **SUPERPOST**

Quick ¹..... !
We get your parcel to the USA or Europe the next day.

Free ²..... !
We come to your office to pick up your parcel.

Free ³..... !
If we lose or break your parcel, we'll pay you up to £5,000 per item.

No ⁴..... !
You can send as many kilos as you want.

2.2 Match the adjectives with the nouns they can describe.

Adjectives	Nouns
1 convenient	a) delivery
2 fast	b) parcel
3 expensive	c) service
4 good	d) insurance cover
5 high	e) weight limit
6 quick	
7 heavy	

3 Language Focus A

Janet Parker of Wilcox International telephones an assistant at Interpack.

3.1 ▦ Listen and complete the table with details about Superpost, one of Interpack's services.

	Worldpost	Superpost
Delivery time		
USA/Europe	from 5 days	1
rest of the world	from 10 days	2
Weight limit?	yes, 30 kg	3
Insurance cover per parcel	up to £250	4
Do they collect?	no	5
Sample costs		
5 kg to Germany	£18.20	6
5 kg to Japan	£30.90	7
Countries	230	8

3.2 What are the missing words? Use the information in 3.1 and the adjectives in 2.2 to help you.

Example: 1 = faster

1 We use Worldpost at the moment, but we sometimes need a ..... service.
2 You could try Superpost. The delivery is ..... than Worldpost.
3 Can you send parcels ..... than 30 kg?
4 The insurance cover is .... Worldpost: up to £5,000 per parcel.
5 That's .... than going to your office.
6 Of course, Superpost is ..... expensive ..... Worldpost.
7 Superpost takes ..... time.
8 Worldpost covers ..... countries.

3.3 ▦ Listen again. Are your words the same as the words on the cassette?

5 Practice

5.1 How do these adjectives change when you compare two things?

1 cheap	6 small
2 high	7 practical
3 big	8 low
4 efficient	9 attractive
5 slow	10 heavy

5.2 Look again at the types of communication in the Preview. Compare letters and faxes. Use these words.

Adjectives	Nouns
fast	time
convenient	money
cheap	
expensive	

5.3 Work with a partner.
Student A: Look at page 114.
Student B: Complete the table with the information your partner gives you about ICS's Jetmail service.

Jetmail	

Delivery time
  USA/Europe
  rest of the world
	
	1
	2

Weight limit?	3
Insurance cover per parcel	4
Do they collect?	yes

Sample costs
  5 kg to Germany
  5 kg to Japan
	
	£42.50
	£62.20

Countries	190

5.4 Now tell your partner about ICS Jetmail's collection, sample costs and countries.

5.5 Compare Worldpost and Jetmail. Talk about these points.

1 delivery	3 cost
2 insurance cover	4 countries covered

5.6 Compare Jetmail and Superpost.

Comparatives – looking at two things

ADJECTIVES

fast – faster	big – bigger
quick – quicker	heavy – heavier

good – better

bad – worse

convenient – more convenient

expensive – more expensive

We sometimes need a **faster** service.
The insurance cover is **better** than Worldpost.
Superpost is **more expensive than** Worldpost.

NOUNS

Superpost takes **less** time **than** Worldpost.
Worldpost covers **more** countries.

CHECK!

1 **When do you use er at the end of an adjective?**
2 **When do you use more before an adjective?**
3 **Which word is missing from these sentences?**
   a) Faxes are more expensive . . . . . letters.
   b) Faxes are faster . . . . . letters.

4 Speechwork

🖳 **Listen to these sentences. What sound do you hear in the underlined parts?**

1 We need a fas<u>ter</u> service.
2 The insurance cover is bet<u>ter</u> th<u>an</u> Worldpost.
3 Superpost is more expensive th<u>an</u> Worldpost.

6 Language Focus B

6.1 Look at the complete table. Are the sentences below true or false?

	Worldpost	Superpost	Jetmail
Delivery time USA/Europe rest of the world	from 5 days from 10 days	next day 2 days	1–3 days up to 4 days
Insurance cover	up to £250	up to £5,000	up to £1,000
Sample costs 5 kg to Germany 5 kg to Japan	£18.20 £30.90	£39.80 £88.40	£42.50 £62.20
Countries	230	160	190

	True	False
1 Jetmail is the quickest service.	☐	☐
2 Jetmail takes the least time to the USA.	☐	☐
3 Superpost offers the best insurance cover.	☐	☐
4 Worldpost is the cheapest service.	☐	☐
5 For parcels to Germany, Superpost is the most expensive.	☐	☐
6 Worldpost covers the most countries.	☐	☐

6.2 Now correct the false sentences.

LANGUAGE SUMMARY B

Superlatives – looking at three or more things
ADJECTIVES
the quickest   the best   the most expensive
the cheapest   the worst

Worldpost is **the cheapest** service.
Superpost is **the most expensive**.

NOUNS
Superpost takes **the least** time.
Worldpost covers **the most** countries.

CHECK!

What is the superlative form of these adjectives?
heavy   practical   slow   high   convenient

7 Practice

7.1 Look at the table in 6.1 again and answer these questions.

1 Which service is the slowest?
2 Which service is the most expensive for parcels to Japan?
3 Which service has the lowest insurance cover?
4 Which service takes the least time to Europe?

7.2 Which service would you choose for these companies and why?

1 This company sends 30 to 40 10 kg parcels to Germany each week. The parcels are not urgent.
2 This company sometimes needs to send very expensive components to the USA quickly. The components break easily.
3 This company sends small parcels to Japan once a week. The Head Office in Japan needs to receive the parcels in less than five days.

8 Output

8.1 What makes your company or its products and services special? Think of seven points which make you different from your competitors.

8.2 Compare your company or its products and services with one of your competitors. Present your ideas.

Working Practices

1 Preview

1.1 What country do you think these people come from?

1.2 Is it the same in your country?

As a manager, I get four weeks holiday per year, but I only take two weeks.

In my company, nobody stays in the office after 4.00 p.m. on Friday.

In my country, only about 5 per cent of company directors are women.

I eat my main meal in the company canteen at lunch. In the evening I just have a light meal.

2 Language Focus

The table has information about four PBX subsidiaries in different countries.

	Working day	Percentage of people who go home for lunch	Average spent on lunch	Time spent on lunch
France	9.00–18.00	3%	£2.68	80% = <1 hour 20% = 1–2 hours
Germany	8.00–16.30	3%	£1.74	87% = <1hour 13% = 1–2 hours
Italy	8.30–18.30	45%	£2.41	49% = <1 hour 51% = 1–2 hours
UK	9.00–17.30	26%	£1.30	92% = <1 hour 8% = 1–2 hours

Use the information in the table to complete these sentences.

1 Eighty-seven per cent of employees in ..... spend less than an hour on lunch.
2 The employees of ..... spend the least money on lunch.
3 The subsidiary with the longest working day is ..... .
4 The same percentage of people go home for lunch in Germany and ..... .
5 The working day in PBX France is not as long as it is in ..... .
6 The employees of ..... take the shortest lunch breaks.
7 PBX employees in ..... and ..... start work at the same time, but in ..... they finish earlier.

LANGUAGE SUMMARY

Comparing

The working day in	PBX France is not as long as in PBX Italy. PBX Italy is longer than in PBX France.

Showing similarity

The same percentage of people go home for lunch in France and Germany. PBX employees in the UK and France start work at the same time.

CHECK!

1 **When do you use as?**
2 **When do you use than?**
3 **Put as or than in these sentences.**
  a) Our lunch break is longer ..... yours.
  b) Our working day is not ..... long ..... yours.

The working week

People in PBX Germany and PBX UK work [1] ..... , but people in the German subsidiary start and finish work [2]..... .

Lunch

The average cost of lunch in the canteen is [3] ..... in PBX UK than in PBX Germany, but in PBX UK a [4]..... people have lunch out. Most people in PBX Germany and the UK take a lunch break of [5]..... one hour.

The extract above is from a report on working practices. It compares PBX Germany and PBX UK.

3 Practice

3.1 Complete the extract with these words.

a) higher percentage of people
b) lower
c) less than
d) an hour earlier
e) the same number of hours

3.2 Look at the table in 2 again. Compare the four different subsidiaries. Talk about these points.

1 the working day –
  compare Germany with the UK
2 the time spent on lunch –
  compare Germany with Italy
3 when people finish work –
  compare France with Italy
4 the money spent on lunch –
  compare Italy with France

4 Numberwork

4.1 Match the symbols and the expressions.

Example: 1 = c

Symbols	Expressions
1 <10	a) ten per cent
2 5–10	b) from five to ten per cent
3 10%	
4 >10	c) less than ten
5 5–10%	d) more than ten
	e) between five and ten

NUMBERWORK SUMMARY

You see	You say
<5	less than five
>5	more than five
2–5	two to five *or* between two and five

4.2 Work with a partner. Look at the table in 2 again. Take turns to ask and answer questions about the time people spend on lunch.

Model

A How long do people in PBX Germany spend on lunch?

B Eighty-seven per cent spend less than an hour.
   Thirteen per cent spend between one and two hours.

5 Wordwork

Complete the list.

Nouns	Adjectives
informality	informal
punctuality	1 . . . . .
2	popular
similarity	3 . . . . .
difference	different
4	important
attraction	attractive
competition	5 . . . . .
reputation	reputable
fashion	6 . . . . .
culture	cultural
agriculture	7 . . . . .

6 Listening

Two people are talking about working conditions in the Netherlands.

Listen and complete part A of the table.

	A Netherlands B Ireland C Greece D Your country
Working hours	
Extra work	
Holidays	
Punctuality	
Entertaining	
Women in business	

7 Reading

Student A: Look at page 114.
Student B: Read the report on Ireland and complete part B of the table.

Working around the world – Ireland

Working hours

Official business hours are from 9.00 a.m. to 5.00 or 5.30 p.m., but many factories start at 8.00 a.m. or earlier. In fact, Irish managers often begin early and stay late in the evenings. Most managers take four or five weeks holiday, usually two weeks in July or August, a week at Christmas and some time at Easter.

Punctuality

In the past Ireland did not have a good reputation for punctuality. But now people are usually punctual for business appointments and meetings. However in social situations punctuality is of less importance.

Entertaining

Lunch is the most popular way of entertaining clients in Ireland. Business lunches often take place in an informal setting such as a pub.

Women in business

Women today have a better position in business than before. Many women have good jobs in finance, marketing, buying and selling, law and the fashion industry.

8 Speaking

8.1 Work with a partner. Answer his or her questions about Ireland.

8.2 Ask your partner about Greece and complete part C of the table.

9 Output

9.1 Complete part D of the table with information about your country.

9.2 Compare your country with one of the other countries in the table. Present your ideas.

Discussions

1 Preview

Read this memo. What suggestions do you have?

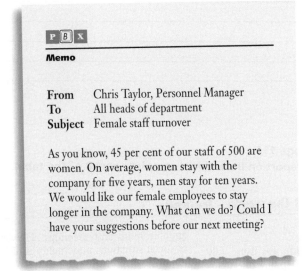

> **PBX**
>
> **Memo**
>
> **From**   Chris Taylor, Personnel Manager
> **To**   All heads of department
> **Subject** Female staff turnover
>
> As you know, 45 per cent of our staff of 500 are
> women. On average, women stay with the
> company for five years, men stay for ten years.
> We would like our female employees to stay
> longer in the company. What can we do? Could I
> have your suggestions before our next meeting?

2 Wordwork

Read these suggestions from the heads of department of PBX UK. Replace the underlined words with one of these expressions.

Example: 1 = b

a) career breaks   d) flexitime
b) crèche   e) part-time work
c) teleworking

1 Set up a <u>centre to look after our employees' small children</u> in the company.
2 Offer our employees <u>jobs for only part of the day or the week</u>.
3 Introduce <u>a system where people can leave their job for some years then come back to it later</u>.
4 Introduce <u>a system where people get computers and can work from home</u>.
5 Introduce <u>a system where people can start and leave work at different times</u>.

3 Language Focus

Chris Taylor, Pat March (Head of PBX's Accounts Department) and John Beatty (Head of PBX's Computer Services Department) are talking about the suggestions in 2.

3.1 🔊 Listen to their conversation and answer these questions.

1 Which three suggestions do they discuss?
2 Which two suggestions are possible solutions to the problem?

3.2 🔊 Listen again. Are these sentences true or false? How do you know?

	True	False
1 Pat likes the suggestion of a crèche.	☐	☐
2 John doesn't like this suggestion.	☐	☐
3 Pat doesn't like the suggestion of career breaks.	☐	☐
4 John agrees with Pat about career breaks.	☐	☐
5 Pat changes her mind about career breaks.	☐	☐
6 John likes the suggestion of teleworking.	☐	☐
7 Pat likes this suggestion too.	☐	☐
8 Chris doesn't think teleworking is a good idea for every department.	☐	☐

You ask what people think
What do you think about setting up a crèche?

You like a suggestion
A crèche is an excellent idea.
I like the idea.
I think it's a possible solution.
I think it's a good solution.

You don't like a suggestion
I don't think career breaks are a good idea for us.

You agree with another person
I agree.
I agree with Pat.
Yes, you're right.

You agree, but not 100 per cent
That's true, but staff from some departments can't work from home.

You don't agree with another person
I don't really agree.

4 Speechwork

📼 **Listen to three ways of saying this sentence. What does each speaker think?**

> I don't think career breaks are a good idea for us.

...but they are a good idea for other companies

1 ☐ 2 ☐ 3 ☐

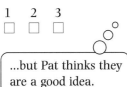

...but Pat thinks they are a good idea.

1 ☐ 2 ☐ 3 ☐

...but another suggestion is a good idea.

1 ☐ 2 ☐ 3 ☐

5 Practice

Alan, Brenda and Charles also work for PBX.
They are discussing PBX's canteen.

5.1 Complete their discussion with expressions from the Language Summary.

ALAN I think we should close the company canteen. Only 50 per cent of the employees use it and it costs a lot of money.

BRENDA ¹. . . . . I think we need to make the food better. Then more people would use it.

CHARLES ². . . . . The food is terrible. That's why I don't use the canteen. ³. . . . . asking an external catering company to run our canteen? I know Keatings did that and their canteen is very successful now.

BRENDA ⁴. . . . . It's a good way to cut the company's costs and have better food too.

ALAN ⁵. . . . . employees often pay more for their food.

5.2 Work with a partner. Think about your organisations. What are some reasons for and against these suggestions?

1 introducing teleworking
2 introducing flexitime
3 introducing career breaks
4 introducing part-time work

5.3 Work in groups of four. Discuss the suggestions in 5.2. Take turns to be A, B, C and D.

Conversation Plan
A Choose one suggestion. Ask what B thinks about it.
B Show you like the suggestion. Give reasons.
C Show you don't like the suggestion. Give reasons.
D Agree with B or C. Give reasons.

6 Tactics Focus

🎧 Listen again to 3.1. At the end of each point, Chris summarises the discussion. What does she say about
1 a crèche?   2 career breaks?   3 teleworking?

TACTICS SUMMARY

When you lead discussions, summarise people's feelings at the end of each point.
So you think that a crèche is one solution.
So it seems that career breaks are not practical for PBX.
So you like the idea, but I think we need to talk to more departments.

7 Practice

7.1 🎧 **Listen to three discussions. Which sentence describes which discussion?**

	1	2	3
Everyone in the discussion likes this suggestion.	☐	☐	☐
People don't agree with each other about this suggestion.	☐	☐	☐
Nobody in the discussion likes this suggestion.	☐	☐	☐

7.2 🎧 **Listen again. Choose a summary for each discussion from this list.**
So we agree that flexitime is a good idea.
So you think that a crèche is a possible solution.
So you like the idea, Brenda, but Alan thinks we need more information about food prices.
So you don't think this is a good idea for us.
So Brenda likes the idea, but you think it's not practical for your department.

7.3 🎧 **Now listen to the end of these discussions. Are your summaries the same as the summaries on the cassette?**

7.4 Work in groups of three. Take turns to be A, B and C. Discuss these points.
1 banning smoking in all parts of the company
2 offering language classes to all employees in the company
3 setting up a centre for video conferences in the company
Conversation Plan
A Ask what B thinks.
B Show you like/don't like this suggestion. Give reasons.
C Show you agree/don't agree with B. Give reasons.
A Summarise the feelings of B and C.

8 Output

8.1 Work in groups. Think of four suggestions to improve the quality of life in your workplace.

8.2 Choose two of these suggestions for more discussion.

8.3 One person from your group takes your two suggestions to another group. This person leads a discussion about your two suggestions. He/she uses the role card your teacher gives him or her.

Restaurants

1 Preview

Think about another country you know well. What is different about

the restaurants?   the food?   the way the food is served?

2 Wordwork

2.1 Put these foods in the groups below.

Examples: anchovy = fish   chicken = poultry

anchovy   chicken   cream   duck   garlic   ham   lamb   leek
lettuce   melon   mushroom   onion   orange   potato   prawn
salmon   steak   veal

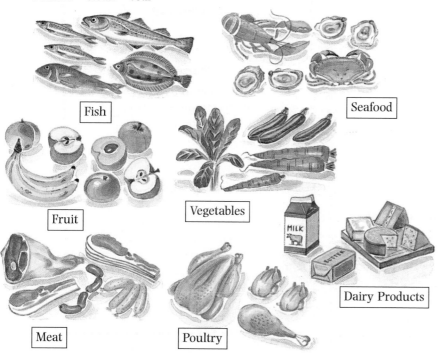

Fish

Seafood

Fruit

Vegetables

MILK

Dairy Products

Meat

Poultry

2.2 The verbs on the left are different methods of cooking food. Match the verbs and the meanings.

Example: 1 = d

Verbs	Meanings
1 bake	a) cook in the oven with some extra oil or fat
2 boil	b) cook in a pan with some oil or fat
3 fry	c) cook with a strong direct heat over or under the food
4 grill	d) cook in the oven but with no extra oil or fat
5 roast	e) cook in a pan with very hot water

2.3 How can you cook these foods?

1 a duck   4 mushrooms
2 eggs   5 potatoes
3 a hamburger   6 a steak

3 Language Focus

Patrick Mulligan from Keatings and Maurizio Rivella from Pastificio Rivella are in a restaurant.

3.1 🖵 Listen to their conversation and answer these questions.

1 What does Maurizio choose as a starter?
2 What does Maurizio choose as a main course?

3.2 🖵 Listen again. What do they say?

1 Patrick asks Maurizio what he wants as a starter.
2 Maurizio asks Patrick to recommend a starter.
3 First Patrick recommends the grilled prawns.
4 Then he recommends the leek and potato soup.
5 Maurizio accepts Patrick's second recommendation.
6 Patrick asks Maurizio what he wants as a main course.
7 Maurizio says what he wants.

Discussing a menu

QUESTIONS

What would you like as a | starter?
| main course?
| dessert?

What do you recommend?

ANSWERS

I'll | have | the | soup.
| try | | steak.
| | | melon.

Why don't you try the grilled prawns?
You could try the soup.

CHECK!

Choose the correct answer.
1 What would you like as a starter?
   a) You could try the soup?
   b) I'll try the soup.
2 What do you recommend?
   a) Why don't you try the soup.
   b) I'll have the soup.

4 Speechwork

4.1 🔲 Listen and repeat these words.

1 fish   3 ham
2 leek   4 duck

4.2 🔲 Listen. Tick the word which has the same sound as the underlined part.

		fish	leek	ham	duck
1	chicken	✔	☐	☐	☐
2	cream	☐	☐	☐	☐
3	grilled	☐	☐	☐	☐
4	lamb	☐	☐	☐	☐
5	mushroom	☐	☐	☐	☐
6	onion	☐	☐	☐	☐
7	salad	☐	☐	☐	☐
8	veal	☐	☐	☐	☐

5 Practice

Work with a partner. Look at the menu and have conversations. Take turns to be A and B.

Model
A What would you like as a starter?
B I'll try the . . . . . , please.
A And for the main course? What would you like?
B What do you recommend?
A You could try the . . . . . .
B I'm not very keen on . . . . . .
A Well, why don't you try the . . . . . ?
B That sounds good. I'll try that.

The
CELLAR
Restaurant

Lunch Menu

Starters

Melon with ham
Grilled prawns with garlic
Seafood salad
Leek and potato soup
Fish soup

Main courses

Roast chicken
Duck in an orange sauce
Salmon in a cream sauce
Steak in a pepper sauce
Escalope of veal

6 Tactics Focus

6.1 🔲 Listen to three conversations. Which conversation is about

	1	2	3
a main course?	☐	☐	☐
an Indonesian salad?	☐	☐	☐
a seafood starter?	☐	☐	☐

6.2 🔊 **Listen again. What are the missing words?**

GADO-GADO

That's an . . . . . . It's a salad of . . . . . and hard-boiled eggs. It's served cold with . . . . . . It's unusual, but . . . . . .

JANSSON'S FRESTELSE

It's made with . . . . . . It's baked . . . . . . It's a simple dish but . . . . . .

SHRIMP COCKTAIL

Shrimps are similar to . . . . . . And shrimp cocktail is . . . . . in a pink sauce similar to mayonnaise. It's served with . . . . . .

TACTICS SUMMARY

Foreign guests may not know very much about the food in your country or region. When you describe dishes

- Tell your guest what the **main** ingredients are and how the dish is cooked and served.
  It's made with potatoes, onions, anchovies and cream.
  It's a salad of cooked, green vegetables.
  It's baked in the oven.
  It's served with a special peanut sauce.
- Compare the dish with food which your guest knows.
  Shrimps are similar to prawns.

7 Practice

Work with a partner. Think of a dish and describe it. Explain where it's from and how it's cooked and served. Your partner must try to guess the name of the dish.

8 Output

8.1 Write a short menu with three starters and three main courses. Include some unusual dishes from your country or region.

8.2 How can you describe the unusual dishes to a visitor? Complete the table.

Made with	
Served with	
Similar to	
How it's cooked	

8.3 Work with a partner and have conversations.

Roles	Take turns to be the host and the visitor.
Place	In a restaurant in your town.

LEARNING TIP

🔊 **Look at the cartoon and listen to the cassette. Why does the waitress say What?!?**

1 Is correct pronunciation important? Put a number from 1–5 (1 = very important, 5 = not very important) to show how important it is for you when you
  a) speak to native speakers of English. ☐
  b) speak to other people in English. ☐
2 When is it important to have correct pronunciation? Put a number from 1–5 to show how important it is when you
  a) are abroad and have to do things in English (e.g. change money). ☐
  b) speak on the telephone. ☐
  c) meet a person for the first time. ☐
  d) talk to people in a social situation. ☐
  e) talk to strangers (e.g. you ask for directions in the street). ☐
  f) talk to your customers and clients. ☐
  g) talk to other people in your organisation. ☐

- Correct pronunciation is very important when you speak to native speakers who don't often meet foreigners.
- Other native speakers and non-native speakers are usually tolerant of incorrect pronunciation.
- In some situations (e.g. in 2a, b, c, e and f above), correct pronunciation is very important.

A New Office

1 Listening

Alison Keiler is a director of Ace Advertising, a small advertising agency. The company is planning to move into an old warehouse and to convert it into an office.

📺 **Listen to a phone call between Alison Keiler and an architect, Ian Brown, and answer these questions.**

1 Is this the first contact between Alison Keiler and Ian Brown?
2 How do you know?
3 Why is Alison telephoning Ian?
   a) to offer him work
   b) to arrange a meeting
   c) to invite him for lunch
4 What do they arrange?
   Complete the table.

Date	
Time	
Activity	
Meeting place	

2 Wordwork

Complete the list.

Adjectives	Comparative forms
good	1 . . . . .
2	worse
easy	3 . . . . .
4	more efficient
comfortable	5 . . . . .
6	more attractive
quiet	7 . . . . .
8	more difficult
interesting	9 . . . . .

3 Speaking

3.1 Look at Ian Brown's plans for Ace Advertising's new office.

3.2 Work with a partner. Make sentences comparing offices like the ones in 3.1. Use words from 2.

Example: Offices like plan 1 are quieter.

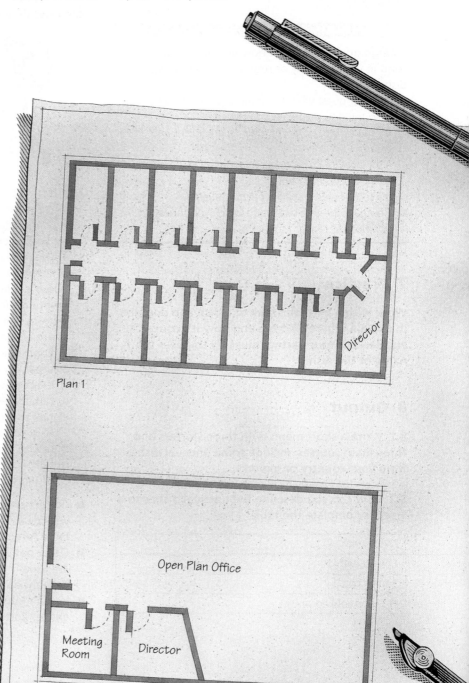

Plan 1

Director

Open Plan Office

Meeting Room

Director

Plan 2

3.3 Work in groups of three. You all work for Ace Advertising. Discuss the two suggestions for the layout of your new office.

Conversation Plan

A Ask what B thinks about plan 1.

B Show you like/don't like this suggestion. Give reasons.

C Show you agree/don't agree with B. Give reasons.

A Summarise the feelings of B and C. Then ask what C thinks about plan 2.

B Show you like/don't like this suggestion. Give reasons.

C Show you agree/don't agree with C. Give reasons.

A Summarise the feelings of B and C.

BROWN & HAY
ARCHITECTS
~: *Proposal* :~

For : Ace Advertising

Location : Offices at Riverside Road

Staff : Director and fifteen employees

Plan 1 Cost £100,000

Plan 2 Cost £65,000

4 Reading

4.1 Student A: Look at page 114.
Student B: Read this extract from a brochure about office machines and make notes in part B of the table.

X50 FAX

The X50 Fax is designed for use in busy offices. It is available in grey or cream. It has a 16-number memory for quick and easy dialling. You can fax up to five A4 sheets automatically. It uses a roll of paper. The roll is 210mm wide and 100m long.

With our faxes you can
- avoid postal delays
- communicate quickly and efficiently
- send or receive faxes anywhere in the world

| Price | £549.00 |

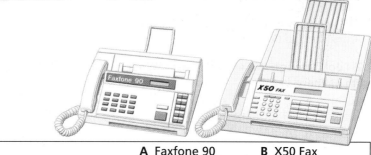

	A Faxfone 90	**B** X50 Fax
For use in		
Choice of colour		
Special features		
Paper roll dimensions		
Price		

4.2 Work with a partner. Tell him or her about the X50 Fax.

4.3 Your partner tells you about the Faxfone 90. Make notes in part A of the table.

5 Speaking

5.1 You want this information about Ace Advertising. What questions can you ask about

1 the number of faxes they receive per day?
2 the amount of money they can spend on a fax machine?
3 the number of clients they fax?

5.2 Ask your teacher the questions.

5.3 Work with a partner. Which fax machine should Ace Advertising buy? Why?

25

Developments

1 Preview

Think about your life, your job and your city a year ago. Think about the situation now. Talk about the changes in this period.

2 Language Focus A

2.1 Read the extracts from Wilcox International's company magazine and answer these questions.

1 Do you know **exactly** when Wilcox opened a sales office in China?
2 Do you know **exactly** when Alec Macfarlane transferred to Germany?

2.2 Look through the extracts again. What is the form of these verbs?

1 be	4 go up	7 return
2 begin	5 set up	8 rise
3 build	6 transfer	

LANGUAGE SUMMARY A

Present perfect: verb be
The last twelve months **have been** very successful.

Present perfect: regular verbs
We **have opened** a sales office in China.

Alec Macfarlane	has	**transferred** to Germany.
Jim Lake		**returned** to Head Office.

Present perfect: irregular verbs
We **have set up** a subsidiary in Germany.
The company **has built** 200 offices.
Turnover from our foreign operations **has risen**.

Present perfect: negative
Turnover **has not gone up** in the UK.

CHECK!

1 **When do you use the present perfect?**
2 **Put these verbs in the present perfect.**
   a) In the last year profits (rise).
   b) In the last six months the company (expand).
   c) Over the last two months costs (not go up).

Achievements this year

The last twelve months have been very successful for Wilcox International.

In the last twelve months we have
- set up a subsidiary in Germany.
- built 200 offices for eighty different clients.
- opened our first sales office in China.

At Head Office work has begun on a new administrative building and

3 Speechwork

🔊 **Listen. What happens to the underlined words?**

1 <u>They</u> <u>have</u> opened an office in China.
2 <u>We</u> <u>have</u> set up a subsidiary in Germany.
3 Turnover <u>has</u> <u>not</u> gone up in the UK.
4 Jim <u>Lake</u> <u>has</u> returned to Head Office.

4 Practice

4.1 Work with a partner. Look at the information about Lee-Pack, an American company. How well has it done this year? Take turns to ask and answer questions.

	Last year	This year
Turnover	$5,120m	$4,950m
Number of employees	13,000	13,000
Market share in the US	45%	42%
Number of sales offices abroad	30	36

Model
A What's happened to turnover?
B It's gone down.

On the move

■ Alec Macfarlane has transferred to our new subsidiary in Germany, as General Manager.

■ Jim Lake has returned to Head Office after several years with Wilcox Japan.

Financial results

Turnover from our foreign operations has risen because of an expansion of our activities in South America and South-East Asia. Turnover has not gone up in the UK. This is because

4.2 Work with a partner. Think about the last three months. Tell your partner about

three things you've done.
three things which have happened in your town.
three important developments in your country.

5 Language Focus B

Ann Dixon, Editor of Wilcox International's company magazine, telephones Jack Nolan, General Manager at Wilcox Far East.

5.1 ▣ Listen and tick the correct answer.

		Yes	No
1	successful year?	✓	☐
2	turnover up?	☐	☐
3	profits up?	☐	☐
4	the markets?	Good	Bad
	a) Japan?	☐	☐
	b) Hong Kong?	☐	☐

5.2 What questions can you ask to get this information about Wilcox Far East?

1 successful year   3 profits up
2 turnover up   4 Japan

5.3 ▣ Listen again. Are your questions the same as the questions on the cassette?

LANGUAGE SUMMARY B

Present perfect: Yes/No questions

QUESTIONS	ANSWERS
Has turnover **gone up**?	Yes, it **has**.
Have profits **gone up**?	No, they **haven't**.

Present perfect: open questions
What**'s happened** in Japan?

CHECK!

Make questions. Put these words in the correct order.
1 a successful year/been/has/it?
2 in/what's/the US market/happened?

6 Wordwork

6.1 Complete the points of the compass.

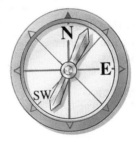

6.2 Work in groups. Think of two countries in each of these areas.

Example: Kuwait is in the Middle East.

The Middle East   The Caribbean
The Far East   South-East Asia
Central America   Northern Europe
Southern Africa   Australasia
North Africa   Central Asia

7 Practice

**7.1 Work with a partner.
Student A: Look at page 115.
Student B: Ask your partner
questions. Complete the
information about Wilcox
South-East Asia's performance
this year.**

Wilcox South-East Asia – Update

Financial overview

Successful year? Yes/No
Turnover up? Yes/No (.....%)
Profits up? Yes/No (.....%)

Changes and developments in the main markets

Singapore .....
Malaysia .....

**7.2 Use this information about
Wilcox North America to answer
your partner's questions.**

Wilcox North America – Update

Financial overview

Not a very good year
– turnover down (15%)
– profits down (6%)

Changes and developments in the main markets

USA – closed our sales offices in
Miami and San Francisco
Canada – won a contract to
build a hospital

**7.3 Write a fax to Ann Dixon. Explain what has happened in Wilcox
South-East Asia. Use the information your partner gave you.**

Facsimile

Wilcox
International

To: .....
From: .....

Subject: This year's results in Wilcox South-East Asia

Financial results
This year .....

Changes and developments in the main markets

8 Output

**8.1 What has happened in your company, department or
organisation over the last six months? Make notes of any new
words.**

**8.2 Work with a partner. Ask and answer questions about your
companies, departments or organisations.**

26

Progress Reports

1 Preview

John Beatty is organising a conference at PBX, Birmingham. It is the end of March and he is on time with his plans.

Look at the activity plan and talk about his progress.

	Jan	Feb	Mar	Apr	May	Jun	Jul
Contact speakers	██	██					
Book hotel		▪					
Prepare programme			██	██	█		
Invite delegates				██	██	█	

Now

2 Wordwork

2.1 These words are about recruitment. Complete the sentences with words from this list.

Example: 1 = a

a) advertisement
b) candidates
c) schedule
d) application
e) interviews
f) short-list

> **Urgently required**
> ## Commercial Manager
> Knowledge of and experience in marketing skills essential, also knowledge of

1 This is a job . . . . . .

Dear Sirs

I am writing to apply for the post of Commercial Manager as advertised recently in the press.
I enclose a C.V. with details of my experience. As you will see

2 This is a letter of . . . . . .

10.00	Tom Banks
10.45	Sheila Adams
11.30	Brad Hillier
12.15	Lunch

2.2 Listen. How many syllables do you hear?

Example: advertisement =
ad/ver/tise/ment = 4

1 advertisement   5 schedule
2 application   6 short-list
3 candidates   7 recruitment
4 interviews

2.3 Listen again. Underline the stressed syllables.

Example: ad<u>ver</u>tisement

2.4 Which verbs and nouns can go together?

Verbs	Nouns
1 book	a) an advertisement
2 hold	b) an application
3 make	c) a room
4 order	d) coffee
5 place	e) an interview
6 prepare	f) a schedule
	g) a short-list
	h) a flight

Tom Banks
Sheila Adams
Brad Hillier
Kate Harding
John Connor

3 This is a . . . . . with the names of the . . . . . for the job.

4 This is a . . . . . showing the times of the . . . . . .

3 Language Focus

Stanley Tam, a Hong Kong businessman, is planning to open an office in Belgium. He has asked Marianne Boucher to help him recruit local staff. She works for Interconsult in Brussels.

3.1 📼 **Listen to extracts from two phone calls from Stanley Tam to Marianne Boucher. Tick the points on the check-list which are complete.**

Interconsult

Recruitment check-list

Stanley Tam
- Send the text for the job advertisement
- Book a flight to Belgium for the interviews

Marianne Boucher
- Place an advertisement in the newspaper
- Speak to the good candidates on the phone
- Prepare a short-list and send it to Mr Tam
- Choose a date for the interviews
- Book a meeting room for the interviews

3.2 📼 **Listen again. Which sentences tell you if the things on the check-list are complete or not?**

LANGUAGE SUMMARY

Explaining progress: present perfect

| I've / We've | already | spoken to the good candidates. / booked a meeting room. |

| I haven't booked a flight / We haven't prepared the short-list | yet. |

QUESTIONS

| Have you | prepared a short-list yet? / decided where to hold the interviews? |

ANSWERS
Yes, I've already done it.
No, I haven't done that yet.
Not yet.

CHECK!

1 When do you use the adverbs yet and already?

	yet	already
a) with questions	☐	☐
b) with negatives	☐	☐
c) with positives	☐	☐

2 Put yet or already in these sentences.
   a) I've spoken to him about the meeting.
   b) We haven't booked the meeting room.
   c) We plan to close the factory, but we haven't closed it.
   d) Have you finished the report?

4 Practice

Marie Duval of CFI organises training courses. She is organising a leadership course.

4.1 Talk about the things on Marie Duval's check-list.

Leadership Course: Check-list

- Photocopy the course materials ✓
- Book a seminar room at the Royal Hotel ✓
- Book a video camera from the hotel ✗
- Order coffee for the breaks ✓
- Prepare a list of course participants ✗
- Send the participants a map with directions to the Royal Hotel ✗
- Put the course materials in files ✗

Marianne Boucher left this memo for her assistant, David Skinner, two days ago. He has done some of the things on the list but not all of them.

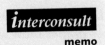

memo

To	David Skinner
From	Marianne Boucher
Subject	Recruitment for Mr Tam

Could you do the following things?

General arrangements
- Phone all the candidates on the short-list to arrange interview times ✓
- Type a schedule for the interviews ✗
- Write to the unsuccessful candidates ✗

Arrangements for the interviews
- Book a room for Mr Tam at the Grand Hotel ✗
- Find out when he is arriving at the airport ✗

Refreshments
- Order coffee at the hotel for the candidates, me and Mr Tam ✓
- Book lunch at the hotel for me and Mr Tam ✓

4.2 Work with a partner. Ask and answer questions to check David's progress.

5 Tactics Focus

Marianne asks her assistant David about progress on the recruitment. She asks her questions in three groups.

🖵 **Listen. Complete the introduction to each group of questions.**

1 . . . . . progress on the recruitment?
2 Now, ... the arrangements for the interviews?
3 And . . . . . , the refreshments.

TACTICS SUMMARY

When you want to ask a lot of questions, try to group them together.
- Introduce each group of questions with a short expression.
  How's progress on the recruitment?
  Now, what about the arrangements for the interviews?
  And one more thing, the refreshments.
- Then ask your specific question.
  Have you typed a schedule for the interviews?
  Have you booked a room for Mr Tam at the Grand?
  Have you ordered coffee at the hotel?

6 Practice

Marie Duval's boss at CFI wants to ask about progress on the leadership course.

6.1 Look at the check-list in 4.1 and group the points.

6.2 Decide

1 what questions to ask.
2 how to introduce each group of questions.

6.3 Work with a partner. One of you is Marie Duval. The other is Marie's boss. Have a conversation about the arrangements for the leadership course.

7 Output

7.1 Write a check-list of things you planned to do this week. Include some things which you have already done and some you haven't done yet.

7.2 Work with a partner. Give him or her your list. Take turns to ask and answer questions about progress.

Business Analysis

1 Preview

1.1 Are products like these popular in your country?

Convenience foods

Snack foods

1.2 Were they popular ten years ago? If not, what has changed, and why?

2 Language Focus

These graphs show sales of four different products.

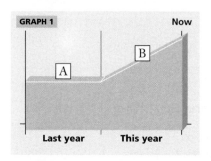

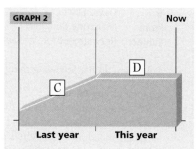

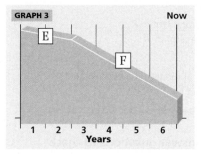

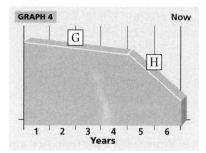

2.1 Match the sentences with the letters on the graphs.

Example: 1 = A

1 Sales remained constant.
2 Sales have remained constant.
3 Sales rose.
4 Sales have risen.
5 Sales fell slightly for two years.
6 Sales fell slightly for four years.
7 Sales have fallen steadily over the last two years.
8 Sales have fallen steadily over the last four years.

2.2 Listen to a description of graphs 1 and 2. Match the trends and the reasons.

Example: 1 = d

Trends	Reasons
1 sales remained constant	a) our advertisements on TV
2 sales have risen	b) competition has increased
3 sales rose	c) a price reduction
4 sales have remained constant	d) the product was not well known

2.3 Listen again. Which two expressions join the trend and the reason?

LANGUAGE SUMMARY

LANGUAGE SUMMARY

Describing change

Sales rose last year.
Sales have risen this year.
Sales fell for two years.
Sales have fallen over the last four years.

Giving reasons

Sales remained constant **because** the product was not well known.
Sales have remained constant **because** competition has increased.
Sales rose **because of** a price reduction.
Sales have risen **because of** our advertisements on TV.

CHECK!

1 When do you use the simple past and when do you use the present perfect?
2 Do you use the simple past or the present perfect with these time expressions?
　a) in 1990　　c) two years ago
　b) this month　d) over the last year
3 When do you use **of** after **because**?
4 How do you join this trend and these reasons?

profits rose { cost reductions
　　　　　　{ we reduced our costs

3 Practice

3.1 Complete the extract from an annual report with these words.

this year　last year　was　has been　has risen
have risen

This year ¹..... very successful for our company. Our total sales ²..... were £20m; ³..... they have risen to £24m. Profits ⁴..... too, from £1.5m to £2m. Last year our market share ⁵..... 12 per cent and this year it ⁶..... to 13.5 per cent.

3.2 What were the trends in your company or organisation last year and this year? Talk about these points.

profits　market share　sales　number of employees

3.3 Join these trends and reasons. Make three sentences for each trend.

Trends	Reasons
1　sales of personal computers rose in the 1980s	they became cheaper
	more people knew how to use them
	children's interest in computer games
2　a lot of companies have introduced teleworking	employees like working from home
	better computer technology
	transport costs have increased

3.4 Give reasons for the trends you talked about in 3.2.

4 Reading

4.1 Work in groups. Your teacher will give you six paragraphs from two different texts. Decide which three paragraphs belong in each text.
Example: 3 = Text 1

4.2 Put the paragraphs in order and choose a title for each one from this list.
Example: 3 = Problem

Problem
Problem and reason
Results
Results and reasons
Solution
Solutions

4.3 Now look at the next page. Are your texts the same?

Text 1

Problem

Europe's market for convenience foods doubled between 1985 and 1991. In 1992, however, sales slowed down all over Europe and even decreased in the mature markets of France, Germany and the UK.

Solution

Because of this, the producers of convenience foods decided to concentrate more on newer markets in Southern Europe, particularly the Italian market.

Results and reasons

Since then, sales in Italy have increased. However, it has not been easy for the producers because Italians have very different eating and shopping habits. For example, they still prefer to buy fresh food in small local shops.

Text 2

Problem and reason

Phileas Fogg is a brand of British snack foods which has been very successful in the UK. However, the company's attempts to enter the European market in the 1980s were unsuccessful because European distribution methods are very different.

Solutions

So, in 1990, they recruited an expert in European marketing. They also changed the products slightly for the European market and redesigned the packaging.

Results

Since then, they have made deals with distributors in the Netherlands, France and Spain and their sales in continental Europe have grown steadily.

4.4 Find words or expressions in the texts with these meanings.

Example: 1 = expert

1 a person who knows a lot about something
2 from that time to now
3 increased, but not as fast as before
4 give more attention to
5 the bags or boxes products come in

5 Writing

5.1 Work in groups. Choose two or three of these products and answer the questions.

large cars   designer clothes   compact discs
cigarettes   fur coats   mobile telephones

1 What happened to sales of these products in the early 1990s?
2 What were the reasons?
3 What did the producers do?
4 What have the results been?

5.2 Complete this paragraph for each product you discussed in 5.1.

In the early 1990s, sales of . . . . . because/because of . . . . . . So the producers decided to . . . . . . Since then, ...

6 Output

6.1 Prepare a short presentation about one of your company's products or services.

Plan

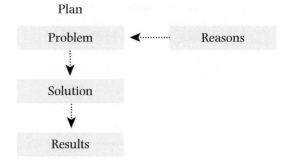

6.2 Now give your presentation.

28

Out and About

1 Preview

When you visit a town you don't know, what do you want to see or do?

		Yes	No
1	go to art galleries	☐	☐
2	go to museums	☐	☐
3	visit historic buildings	☐	☐
4	go to bars and nightclubs	☐	☐
5	try the local food	☐	☐
6	other things	☐	☐

2 Language Focus

2.1 Look at the pictures. Complete the conversations with these questions.

a) What about Alec? Has he gone to Germany yet?

b) What about you? Have you been to New York?

c) Have you been to Madrid before?

2.2 Are these sentences true or false?

	True	False
In picture 1 the speakers are in Madrid.	☐	☐
In picture 2 the speakers are in Germany.	☐	☐
In picture 3 the speakers are in New York.	☐	☐

1   No, it's my first visit here.

2   Yes, he left two weeks ago.

...and then we visited the Statue of Liberty. .....

3   No, but I'd like to go there.

LANGUAGE SUMMARY

Present perfect

QUESTIONS	ANSWERS
Have you been to Madrid before?	No, it's my first visit. Yes, I was here last year.
Has he gone to Germany yet?	No, not yet. Yes, he left two weeks ago.
Have you been to New York?	No, but I'd like to go there. Yes, I was there three years ago.

CHECK!

1 **When do you use been and when do you use gone?**

2 **You are in London on a business trip with a colleague. Which question can you ask?**
   a) Have you been to England?
   b) Have you gone to England?
   c) Have you been to England before?

3 Practice

3.1 Read these questions and answers. Match each question to two possible answers.

Questions	Answers
1 Has Peter been to Japan?	a) Yes, he went there yesterday.
2 Have you been here before?	b) Yes, I think he was there in 1990.
3 Has Luis gone to Madrid yet?	c) No, it's my first visit.
	d) Not yet. He's going tomorrow.
	e) Yes, I have. In fact I lived here for two years.
	f) No, but he's planning to go there next year.

3.2 What questions can you ask in these situations?

1 You and the person you are talking to both know Anna. You know Anna planned to go to live in Korea.
2 You are planning to go to Korea on business. You think your colleague knows Korea.
3 You and a colleague are in Korea on a business trip. You want to know if it is his or her first visit.

4 Conversation Focus

Alec Macfarlane of Wilcox International is in a restaurant in Germany with Wolfgang Binder, the manager of Park and Moss there.

4.1 ▣ Listen to their conversation and answer these questions.

1 Does Alec help the conversation to flow?
2 Does Wolfgang make it clear why Alec should visit Museum Ludwig?

4.2 ▣ Think about these questions.

1 How can Alec help the conversation to flow better?
2 What should Wolfgang say when he suggests Museum Ludwig?

4.3 ▣ Now listen to a second version of their conversation and answer these questions.

1 How does Alec answer these questions?
   a) Have you had time to look round the city?
   b) Have you also been to Museum Ludwig?
2 What does Wolfgang say about Museum Ludwig?

CONVERSATION SUMMARY

When you answer questions in a conversation, don't just answer **yes** or **no**. Try to make comments, give information or ask questions.
My wife and I really like art so we went to the modern art gallery. It has an interesting collection.
Museum Ludwig. No. Where's that?

When people are new to your town or country, suggest places to visit.
You should go to Museum Ludwig. You should go there.

Give some information about the place.
It's in Cologne.
I think it's the best modern art gallery in Germany.
It's not far by train.

5 Practice

5.1 Read the information from the City Guide to Sofia in Bulgaria and complete the table.

1 Place	2 Where it is	3 What makes it special
Alexander Nevski Cathedral	Alexander Nevski Square	
St Sophia Church		It's very old. It has mosaics.
	Knyaz Battenburg Square	

CITY GUIDES

Sofia

On the square

The gold domes of Alexander Nevski Cathedral tower above the city skyline. Visit the cathedral's icons and frescoes. Also see the fifth–sixth century St Sophia Church, with its mosaics, on Alexander Nevski Square. To see Bulgarian art, old and modern, visit the National Art Gallery in Knyaz Battenburg Square.

5.2 Which places in Sofia would you recommend to

1 a visitor who likes art?
2 a visitor who likes historic buildings?

5.3 Work with a partner and have conversations. Use the information in 5.1 and the role cards your teacher gives you.

Model

A Have you been to Sofia before?
B ..... .
A I see. Have you had time to look round the city?
B Not much, but I like ..... so I went to ..... yesterday. I liked the ..... .
A Oh, good. And have you also been to ..... ?
B ..... . No, not yet. Where's that?
A It's in ..... . If you like ..... , you should go there. It ..... .

6 Output

6.1 Think of two or three places in or near your town which visitors often go to. What is special about them? Complete the table.

Place
Where it is
What makes it special

6.2 Work with a partner and have conversations.

Role	Take turns to play the host and the visitor.
Place	In the host's office before a meeting.
Tasks	The host should find out what the visitor has seen and what he/she likes, then suggest other places to visit. The visitor should help the conversation to flow.

29

Present and Future Trends

1 Preview

1.1 Think about your country. Talk about present trends in

population.
sales of products with designer labels.
teleworking.

1.2 Talk about future trends.

2 Language Focus A

These extracts are from an article on present and future trends in Europe.

2.1 Which extract deals with

1 present buying trends?
2 present trends at work?
3 present population trends?

A More and more people are working from home these days. Many large companies, such as Rank Xerox and IBM, have already introduced teleworking for their employees. Small companies are beginning to use teleworking as a way of reducing costs.

B The population of Europe is growing older. People are living longer and the birth rate is falling. At present 20 per cent of the people in the European Union are over sixty years old.

C In the late 1980s, people spent a lot of money on products with designer labels and logos. This has changed. Now people are looking for good quality, not just a famous name.

2.2 Read the extracts again. What are the present trends in

1 working from home?
2 teleworking in small companies?
3 the population of Europe?
4 the length of time people live?
5 the birth rate in Europe?
6 what people want when they buy products?

LANGUAGE SUMMARY A

Describing present trends: present continuous
The population **is growing** older.
People **are living** longer.

CHECK!

1 **Which form of the verb do you use when you talk about present trends?**
2 **Put the verbs in the correct form.**
    a) Companies (recruit) more women these days.
    b) Teleworking (become) very popular now.

3 Practice

3.1 Complete the text with the correct form of these verbs.

become   fall   do   rise

T hese days people are worried about their health. As a result, sales of beer, wine and spirits ¹..... and smoking ²..... unpopular. Sales of health foods ³..... and people ⁴..... more sports.

3.2 Work with a partner. In your country, what are the present trends in

sales of compact discs?   sales of large cars?
house/flat prices?   winter holidays?
the cost of living?

3.3 Look at the photograph. What present trends does it show?

4 Language Focus B

These extracts are from the same article as the article in 2.1. They deal with the same points, but they describe future trends.

4.1 Match these extracts with the extracts in 2.1.

1. This won't change. High quality products will continue to sell well in the future.

2. This trend will continue. The Henley Centre for Forecasting thinks that over ten million people in Britain will work from home in the year 2000.

3. In 2020, 37 per cent will be over sixty. This will be a problem for governments in Europe because there won't be enough young people to pay for the old people's pensions.

4.2 Are the present and future trends for each point the same? Which words tell you?

4.3 Read the extracts again and find the future trends in

teleworking in Britain.
old people's pensions.
sales of high quality products.

LANGUAGE SUMMARY B

Describing future trends with **will**
This trend **will continue**.
High quality products **will continue** to sell well in the future.
This **won't change**.
There **won't be** enough young people to pay for the old people's pensions.

CHECK!

1. **Which form of the verb do you use when you talk about future trends**
   a) in the positive?   b) in the negative?
2. **Change these sentences to describe future trends.**
   a) Companies are recruiting more women these days.
   b) Teleworking is becoming very popular now.

5 Speechwork

⌨ **Listen. What happens to the underlined words?**

1 High quality products are selling well and <u>they</u> <u>will</u> continue to sell well in the future.
2 In 2020, 37 per cent of the population will be over sixty. <u>This</u> <u>will</u> be a problem for governments.
3 The birth rate in Europe is falling. <u>It</u> <u>will</u> continue to fall in the future.
4 This <u>will</u> <u>not</u> change.

6 Practice

6.1 Look at the photographs and answer these questions.

1 What are the current trends in your country for women at work?
2 What do you think will happen in the future?

6.2 Complete this text with **will** or **won't**.

Companies are recruiting more women these days. This [1]..... change. More women [2]..... go out to work and more [3]..... have management positions. As a result, women [4]..... have less time to spend with their families so flexitime and teleworking [5]..... increase. Sales of convenience foods [6]..... rise because women [7]..... have much time for cooking.

6.3 Work with a partner. Have conversations about present and future trends. Take turns to ask and answer questions about these points.

1 the use of English in business
2 the cost of business travel
3 the population of your country
4 teleworking
5 business entertaining

Model
A What do you think are the present trends in .....?
B I think ..... .
A And what do you think will happen in the future?
B I think/don't think it will change. ..... will/won't ..... .
A I agree./I don't really agree. I think ..... .

7 Output

7.1 Think about three trends in your company, department or country. What's happening now? What do you think will happen in the future?

7.2 Present your ideas.

30

Procedures

1 Preview

The pictures show what happens when Keatings introduce a new range of clothes.

Put the pictures in the correct order. Complete the table.

Stage	Picture
1	
2	
3	
4	
5	
6	
7	
8	

A visit/fashion shows

B sign/contract

C choose/wool supplier

D produce/jackets

F choose/manufacturer
draw up/a production schedule

E deliver/to warehouse

H choose/the style and colour
produce/a design brief

G distribute/to stores

2 Language Focus

A buyer is explaining what happens when Keatings introduce a new range of woollen jackets.

2.1 🖳 **Listen. Is the order of stages the same as yours?**

2.2 🖳 **Listen again and complete these sentences.**
1 The design team . . . . . fashion shows.
2 They . . . . . the new style and colours and . . . . . a design brief.
3 After that a wool supplier . . . .
4 I . . . . . the manufacturer. We . . . . . together and . . . . a production schedule.
5 Next the contract . . . . and production . . . . . .
6 The jackets . . . . to our warehouse, and then they're . . . . . to our stores.

2.3 What three expressions does the buyer use to show the order of stages?

LANGUAGE SUMMARY

Describing procedures: simple present active
The designers **choose** the new style.
We **draw up** the production schedule.

Describing procedures: simple present passive
A wool supplier **is chosen**.
The jackets **are delivered** to the warehouse.

Showing the order of stages
After that   Next   Then

CHECK!

1 **Look at the sentences in the Language Summary. Do you know who**
   a) **chooses the new style?**
   b) **chooses the wool supplier?**
   c) **delivers the jackets?**
2 **When do you use the passive form?**
3 **Put the verb choose in the correct form.**
   a) **I . . . . . a manufacturer.**
   b) **A manufacturer . . . . . .**
   c) **Different manufacturers . . . . . for each of our ranges.**
   d) **The buyer . . . . . a manufacturer.**

3 Practice

3.1 Describe what happens when Keatings introduce a new range of jackets. Use the pictures in the Preview on page 99.

3.2 Complete the active and passive forms of these verbs in the simple present.

	Active form	Passive form
choose	choose/chooses	is/are chosen
begin	1	2
build	3	4
order	5	6
send	7	8

4 Wordwork

Which verbs and nouns can go together?

Verbs   Nouns
1 approve   a) staff
2 draw up   b) equipment
3 give   c) plans
4 install   d) permission
5 order
6 present
7 recruit
8 train

5 Reading

5.1 Student A: Look at page 113.
Student C: Look at page 115.
Student B: Read this text and complete 2–5 on the flow-chart.

KEATINGS

A special project team is responsible for finding sites for new Keatings stores. When they have found a suitable site, the company's architects draw up an outline plan for the new store. This is then presented to the Project Planning Committee for approval.

If they approve the plan, it is sent to the local planning authority for building permission. If they give permission, a Project Manager is chosen.

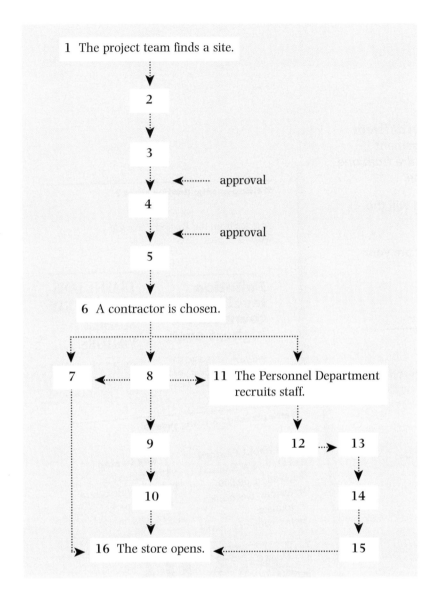

1 The project team finds a site.

2

3

approval

4

approval

5

6 A contractor is chosen.

7   8   11 The Personnel Department
                          recruits staff.

9   12 ... 13

10   14

16 The store opens.   15

6 Speaking

Work in groups of three. Take turns to ask and answer questions. Complete the rest of the flow-chart.

Model
A What happens at stage 2?
B The architects draw up an outline plan.
C What happens after that?

7 Output

7.1 Think about a procedure which is important in your job. What verbs do you need to describe it? Make a list of their active and passive forms.

7.2 Draw a flow-chart to show the different stages in the procedure. Do not complete all the parts.

7.3 Work with a partner. Give him or her your flow-chart and explain your procedure. He/she must complete the flow-chart.

5.2 Read the text again. What do the underlined words refer to?

Example: they in line 2 = the special project team

5.3 These sentences are missing from the text. Where do they go?

1 This shows the size of the store, the position of entrances, exits, escalators and stairs, and the car parking areas.
2 This person is responsible for the project until the opening of the store.

101

31

Solutions

1 Preview

Managers from subsidiaries of PBX in different countries are taking part in a management training programme. These extracts are from one of the simulations on the programme.

1.1 Read the extracts. What problem will the managers discuss?

1.2 Look at the extracts again. What are your ideas and suggestions?

Traffic planning: Briefing sheet 1

You are a team of traffic planning consultants. Your task is to design a plan to improve traffic conditions in Paxford.

Step 1 Information gathering
Objectives:
a) to get information about the problem in Paxford
b) to get information about other towns' solutions to traffic problems

Step 2 First meeting
Objectives:
a) to present the problem in detail
b) to present possible solutions

Step 3 Second meeting
Objectives:
a) to discuss the suggestions from the first meeting
b) to choose one or more solutions
c) to discuss the details and

Traffic planning: Briefing sheet 2

Articles from the *Paxford Chronicle*, May to August 1995

Pollution levels in town centre highest ever

BRENDA ALLWORTHY, Mayor of Paxford, told the Town Council today

TRAFFIC JAMS TERRIBLE, SAY SUMMER VISITORS

RESULTS OF A survey conducted by the Paxford

Traffic planning: Briefing sheet 3

Facts about Paxford
Location: SW England
Population: 60,000
Industries: electronics, tourism
Sights: cathedral, castle

Key to map
✝ = cathedral
▨ = historic centre
P = car park
▢ = business and shopping areas

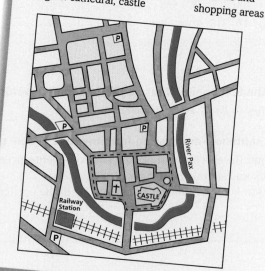

2 Language Focus

Anne, Bill, Carlo and Dagmar, four PBX managers on the training programme, are discussing the problem.

2.1 🖾 Listen to their conversation and number each solution when you hear it.

Solutions	Order
make parking more expensive	☐
make people in cars pay a toll to enter the business and shopping areas	1
build more car parks outside the town	☐
ban traffic from the historic centre	☐

2.2 🖾 Listen again and answer these questions.

1 How does Anne ask for Bill and Carlo's suggestions?
2 How does Bill make his first suggestion?
3 How does Carlo make his first suggestion?
4 How does Anne ask for new ideas?
5 How does Carlo make his new suggestion?
6 How does Bill make his new suggestion?

LANGUAGE SUMMARY

Asking for suggestions
I'd like to hear your suggestions.
Any other ideas?

Suggesting solutions
People in cars **should pay** a toll.
I think we **should ban** traffic from the centre.
We **could make** parking more expensive.
We **could build** more car parks.

CHECK!

Look at these sentences.
I think we should improve public transport.
We could improve public transport.
Which sentence tells you
1 the speaker has thought a lot about his suggestion and feels strongly about it?
2 this is the speaker's new idea?

3 Practice

3.1 Read this problem.
The company's costs are rising and profits are going down.

3.2 What do these people say about this problem? Complete their suggestions.

I want to know what they think.

These ideas are good, but maybe there's another one.

1 I'd like to .....

4 ..... ideas?

I feel strongly about this.

2 Salaries ..... stay at the same levels as last year.

I've studied this. I know it's a good idea.

3 ..... fly economy class, not business class, on sales trips.

5 ..... recruit a new Financial Manager.

3.3 Read this problem and prepare two suggestions.

Your company bans smoking in the office. The company employs fifty telephone sales people. Twelve of them are smokers. They go outside to smoke twice an hour. The non-smokers are unhappy because they have to answer the smokers' telephones when they are outside. The smokers are unhappy because they get cold and wet in winter.

3.4 Work in groups. One person leads a discussion about the problem in 3.3. The leader can suggest solutions too.

4 Tactics Focus

Later in the PBX discussion, Carlo and Dagmar both have an idea to help people with cars who live in the business and shopping areas.

4.1 🖭 Listen and answer these questions.

1 Does Carlo know the words **resident's permit** in English?
2 Does Dagmar know the words **resident's permit** in English?
3 Who is more successful in making the suggestion?
4 Why?

4.2 🖭 Listen again. Which two expressions does Carlo use to show he has an idea but can't find the right words to say it?

When you take part in discussions in English, if you can't find the right words, don't stay silent! Show people that you are thinking or looking for words.
Let me think.
Just a moment.
What do you call it?

5 Practice

Work in groups. Take turns to be the speaker.

SPEAKER You must speak for one minute on a topic your teacher gives you. You mustn't be silent for more than five seconds! Use expressions from the Tactics Summary to show the listeners that you are thinking.

LISTENERS You must interrupt if the speaker is silent for more than five seconds. Then you must speak on the same topic and try to complete the minute.

6 Output

6.1 Work in groups. What are the present or future traffic problems in the town where you live or work? Think of three possible solutions.

6.2 Present your group's ideas and discuss all the possible solutions.

32

Closing Stages

1 Preview

How can you end these conversations?

1 You have finished a successful meeting with one of your suppliers. He/she is flying back to France this evening. Your next meeting is in France in May.

2 You are at the end of a visit to your company's Head Office. Your colleague there arranged a programme of visits for you. It was very useful for you.

3 You are on the phone to a colleague. You are planning a sales meeting. You have finished discussing the programme. You have agreed to fax it to your colleague later today.

2 Conversation Focus

Hong Kong businessman Stanley Tam is at the end of a visit to Belgium to interview candidates for a job. Marianne Boucher of Interconsult in Brussels arranged the interviews for him.

2.1 🖭 Listen to their conversation and complete the table.

	Person
Call with names of successful candidates.	
Phone the successful candidates.	

2.2 🖭 Listen again and answer these questions.

1 What does Marianne say to confirm the actions they have discussed?

2 What does Marianne say to show that the business part of the conversation is finished?

3 What do Stanley and Marianne say to end the conversation politely?

CONVERSATION SUMMARY

Before you end a business conversation

■ Confirm the decisions you have made.
So, we've agreed that you'll call me on Friday with the names of the successful candidates.
I'll phone the successful candidates and offer them the jobs.

■ Show that the business is finished.
I think that's all for now.

■ Thank people for their help.
And thanks for all your help with the arrangements.

■ Wish them a pleasant journey.
Have a good flight back to Hong Kong.

---

3 Practice

You are meeting a colleague to discuss the opening of your company's new office building.

3.1 Work with a partner. Look at the table and decide who will do the actions.

	Person
Invite the mayor to open the building.	
Organise a reception.	
Arrange an interview on local TV for the Managing Director.	

3.2 Now end the meeting. Summarise the actions and who will do them.

4 Speechwork

4.1 🔲 Listen to these words.

1 I'll   3 he'll   5 we'll
2 you'll 4 she'll   6 they'll

4.2 🔲 Listen again. Which of the words in 4.1 do you hear?

Example: 1 = he'll

1 ..... send you a copy of the report.
2 ..... meet him tomorrow.
3 ..... contact you on Monday.
4 ..... arrange a meeting for next week.
5 ..... call you this afternoon.
6 ..... speak to him after lunch.

5 Wordwork

The people in the pictures are ending conversations.

Complete their conversations with these words.

a) give my regards to   c) have a safe trip back
b) I'll be in touch   d) you're welcome

Well, I think it's been a very useful meeting, Mr Nakatane.

Yes, very useful indeed. So ..... to Bratislava.

Thanks. ..... early next week with my comments on the contract.

1

Well, goodbye, Mr Konus. By the way, ... Irena when you get back.

Yes, of course I will.

2

Your taxi's here, Mr Konus.

Good. Well, thanks for all your help, Judy.

....., Mr Konus.

3

6 Practice

Work with a partner. Look again at the Preview on page 105. Have a short conversation for each situation.

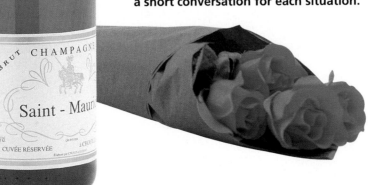

7 Culture Focus

7.1 Answer these questions about your country.

1 When do you give gifts to business contacts and clients?
   a) when they visit your company ☐
   b) when you are on a business trip abroad ☐
   c) at special times of the year ☐
      (e.g. the end of the year, Christmas)
   d) never ☐
   e) at other times ☐

2 If you are on a visit and plan to give a gift, when is the best time to give it?
   a) when you arrive at the company ☐
   b) send it after you get home from your trip ☐
   c) just before you leave the company ☐
   d) at a social event ☐
      (e.g. at lunch after a meeting)
   e) at another time ☐

3 When you give a gift to a business contact do you usually take
   a) a corporate gift ☐
      (e.g. a pen with the company logo)?
   b) something typical from your country? ☐
   c) a personal gift ☐
      (e.g. a CD or cassette for a person who likes music)?
   d) a gift with a designer label? ☐
   e) something else? ☐

4 What kind of gift is most appropriate when you are invited home for dinner during a business trip?
   a) flowers ☐
   b) a present for your host's child/wife/husband ☐
   c) fruit ☐
   d) a bottle of wine ☐
   e) a box of chocolates ☐
   f) something else ☐

5 When is the best time to open a gift?
   a) at the time that you receive the gift ☐
   b) later, in private ☐

7.2 Answer the same questions about another country you know well.

In some cultures, exchanging gifts is very important for good business relationships. Before you give gifts, find out
■ About any special dates when people give gifts. For example, in Japan gifts are given at the end of the year and in July.
■ What kind of gifts are suitable. For example, some kinds of flowers have special meanings in some countries.

8 Practice

A foreigner has come to work in your country. What does he/she need to know about giving gifts?

9 Output

Two important clients are visiting your company next Tuesday. Your boss has asked you to plan an evening programme for them.

9.1 Work in groups. Decide on some details about the visitors (e.g. nationality, age, sex, interests).

9.2 Have a meeting to discuss the evening programme. Use the role cards your teacher gives you.

A Product Launch

1 Grammar Review

Read this extract from a report on the UK bottled water market and answer these questions.

1 When was the report written?
2 Which period does the report cover?
3 Complete the report with the correct form of the verbs.

2 Reading

Look at the graph and complete these sentences.

1 In 1987 consumption was at a level of . . . . . million litres.
2 The following year it rose by . . . . . litres.
3 For the next two years, levels of consumption increased rapidly by . . . . . in 1989 and . . . . . in 1990.
4 The increase continued and at the end of 1992 consumption was at a level of . . . . . .
5 This year it has increased to . . . . . .
6 Levels will continue to increase by around . . . . . a year up to the end of the 90s.

The UK market for bottled water [1]. . . . . (grow) rapidly from 1987–89. Since then, consumption of bottled water [2]. . . . (continue) to rise, but more slowly than before.

The slow-down in the consumption of bottled water in the first two years of the 1990s [3]. . . . . (be) the result of several poor summers and also the severe recession in the UK economy. In this difficult economic period, the supermarkets [4]. . . . . (negotiate) lower prices for bottled water. As a result, the first part of the 90s [5]. . . . . (not be) easy for producers of bottled water.

In the last twelve months, the UK economy [6]. . . . . (begin) to recover. Now consumer confidence [7]. . . . . (return) and consumption of bottled water [8]. . . . . (rise) again. According to the experts, the bottled water market [9]. . . . . (continue) to grow over the next seven years, but at a steadier rate of around 60–70,000 million litres a year.

December 1993

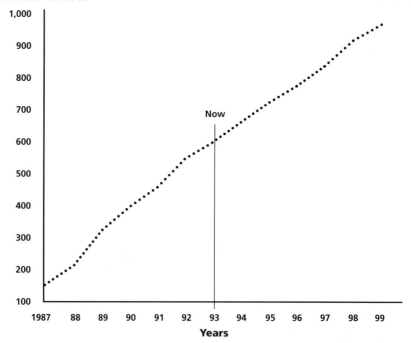

UK bottled water consumption

Millions of litres

Source for data: Zenith International

4 Listening

The Production Manager at Bright Springs is explaining the procedure for packaging and distributing a new range of flavoured bottled water produced in their plant near Matlock.

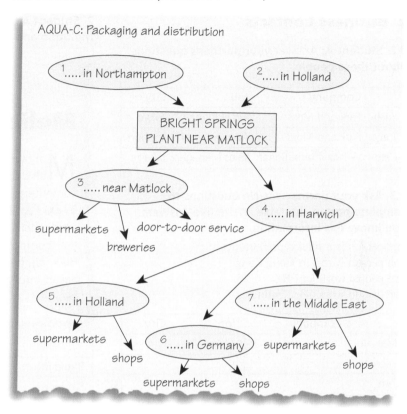

AQUA-C: Packaging and distribution

1 ..... in Northampton
2 ..... in Holland

BRIGHT SPRINGS
PLANT NEAR MATLOCK

3 ..... near Matlock
4 ..... in Harwich

supermarkets
door-to-door service
breweries

5 ..... in Holland
7 ..... in the Middle East

supermarkets
shops
6 ..... in Germany
supermarkets
shops

supermarkets
shops

🔲 **Listen and complete the flow-chart with words from this list.**

Bright Springs' warehouse (x 2)   customers' warehouses (x 3)
bottle factory   printing company

5 Speaking

You work for Bright Springs. The company wants to launch AQUA-C in your country. First they plan to launch the product in your region to test the market.

5.1 Work with a partner. Think of two possible ideas for promoting the product.

5.2 Work in groups of four. You are all employees of the Bright Springs' subsidiary in your country. Have a meeting to discuss your ideas for promoting the launch of AQUA-C.

5.3 Present your group's ideas.

3 Speaking

3.1 Work in groups. Think of three reasons to explain the increase in the consumption of bottled water over the last ten years.

3.2 Present your explanations. Begin

We think consumption of bottled water has risen because/because of
. . . . . .
Another reason/explanation is
. . . . . .

Information for Students A and C

2 Business Contacts

4.2 Student A: Answer your partner's questions about these people.

	Company	Job	City
Yoshi	Park and Moss	Accountant	Tokyo
Tony	Park and Moss	Administrator	London
Kate	Wilcox International	Sales Manager	Jakarta

4.3 Ask your partner Yes/No questions to complete part of the table. Write five answers. You know this information.

one person is a sales representative
one person works in Hong Kong
two people work for PBX
one person works for Keatings

	Company	Job	City
Mary-Jo			
Pablo			
Tim			

Now ask questions with what and where. Complete the rest of the table.

3 Company Information

3.3 Student A: Ask and answer questions to complete the table.

Model
B What do you have in G1?
A 116. What do you have in G2?
B 3,400.

	1	2	3	4
G	116		430	
R	35,000		600,000	
I	650			19,000
D	5,000,000	1,300		

7 Student A: Read the information about Molitano and complete part A of the table.

Molitano

Molitano produces olive oil which it also bottles and sells. It uses a new computerised bottling line and produces 5,000 bottles per hour. Most of its production is for the Italian market, but the company also exports to France, Holland, the UK and Hong Kong. It is based in Sicily and employs eight people.

	A Molitano	B Vinicola Ambra
Based in		
Products		
Production	. . . . . bottles per hour	. . . . . litres per year
Employees		
Main markets		

8.1 Work with a partner. Answer your partner's questions about Molitano.

8.2 Ask questions about Vinicola Ambra and complete part B of the table.

6 City Profiles

5.2 Student A: Answer your partner's questions about costs in Munich and London.

	Hotel	To rent a car
Munich	DM300	DM85 a day
London	£140	£40 a day
New York		
Madrid		

5.3 Now ask your partner questions about costs in New York and Madrid and complete the table in 5.2.

5.4 Answer your partner's questions about the working hours of companies and banks in Belgium.

Working hours in Belgium	
Companies	Mon – Fri: 9.00 a.m. – 12.30 p.m. and 2.30 p.m. – 6.00 p.m.
Banks	Mon – Fri: 9.00 a.m. – 4.00 p.m.
Shops	
Government offices	

5.5 Now ask your partner questions about the working hours of shops and government offices and complete the table in 5.4.

8.1 Student A: Ask questions about Copenhagen. Ask about these points.

office working hours
underground
cost of hotel rooms and car rental
industries

8.2 Now answer B's questions about Amsterdam.

	Amsterdam
Office working hours	8.30 to 5.00
Underground?	yes
Cost of hotel room	400 gilders
Cost of car rental	105 gilders
Industries	brewing, chemicals, shipbuilding

Project Unit: A New Job

2 Student A: Your teacher will give you a fax from Borelec. Read the fax and complete part B of the table.

3.1 Answer your partner's questions about Diamond Electro.

3.2 Ask your partner about Comex and complete part C of the table.

	A Alfacom	B Borelec	C Comex	D Diamond Electro
Business	computer hardware			electronics
Based in	La Défense, Paris			a new town near Nice
Employees	700 in Paris, 12,000 in the world			250 in Nice, 6,000 in the world
Holiday	3 weeks per year			4 weeks per year
Facilities – Sports centre	yes			yes

9 Career Development

8.2 Student A: Jim Lake works for Wilcox International. Ask and answer questions about his career. Complete the table. You start.

	Responsibilities	Dates
Wilcox Canada	Computer Operator	1989–90
Wilcox Malaysia	designing computer systems	
Wilcox Japan		1992–94

11 Past Performance

4.4 Student A: Your partner has information about new car registrations in Finland. Add the information to the graph.

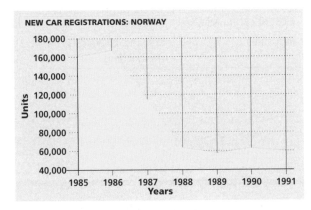

4.5 Your graph also shows new car registrations in Norway. Describe it to your partner. He/she draws your graph.

14 Guidelines

4.1 Student A: Read the article about jet lag. What does it say about time and sleep on long flights? Make notes.

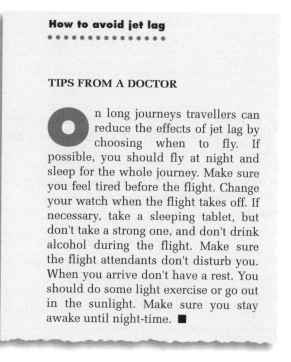

How to avoid jet lag

TIPS FROM A DOCTOR

On long journeys travellers can reduce the effects of jet lag by choosing when to fly. If possible, you should fly at night and sleep for the whole journey. Make sure you feel tired before the flight. Change your watch when the flight takes off. If necessary, take a sleeping tablet, but don't take a strong one, and don't drink alcohol during the flight. Make sure the flight attendants don't disturb you. When you arrive don't have a rest. You should do some light exercise or go out in the sunlight. Make sure you stay awake until night-time. ■

4.2 Work with a partner. What does his or her article say about jet lag? Make notes about food, drink and exercise.

4.3 Tell your partner about the tips in your article.

15 Telephone Calls

7.2 Student A: You work for Garuda Indonesian Airways in Jakarta. A passenger calls you. Find out

1 the passenger's name.
2 the flight number.
3 the destination.
4 the date booked.
5 the date he/she wants to fly.

7.3 You are on business in Milan. You have a ticket for flight AL956 to New York on Thursday morning, but you want to fly the following Tuesday. Phone Alitalia and try to change your flight.

Project Unit: A Top Firm

3 Student A: You work in the Publicity Department at Chupa Chups. Your partner telephones you with some questions about this fax you sent. Answer his or her questions.

> page 2
>
> When his father retired in 1957, Enrique Bernat took over Chupa Chups. At that time the company had more than 200 products. He decided to concentrate on only one product – lollipops. This policy was very successful and sales in Spain increased steadily in the 1960s.
>
> The company began to export its lollipops at the end of the 1960s. Chupa Chups opened its first foreign factory in France in 1969. In 1991 production began at a factory in St Petersburg to supply the Russian market. The United States and Japan are other big markets.
>
> The early 1990s were difficult years for many companies, but Chupa Chups' sales increased by nearly 8 per cent in 1992.
>
> Like many Spanish companies, Chupa Chups is a family business. Enrique Bernat's three sons and one of his daughters work for the company, and his wife is Chupa Chups' Purchasing Manager.

19 Products

4.4 Student A: Ask your partner about the EX-11A and EX-11B coffee makers and complete the table.

	Height	Depth	Width	Cost
EX-11A				
EX-11B				
EX-11C	485mm	580mm	980mm	$3,600
EX-11D	485mm	580mm	1,120mm	$4,300

4.5 Now answer your partner's questions about the EX-11C and EX-11D.

6 City Profiles

8.1 Student C: Listen to A and B. Check the information you hear. Then complete the table.

Model

A What are the working hours of offices in Copenhagen?

B They're from 8.30 to 4.30.

C So 8.30 to 4.30?/So 9.30 to 4.30?

B Yes, that's right./No, that's not quite right. 8.30 to 4.30.

	Copenhagen	Amsterdam
Office working hours		
Underground?		
Cost of hotel room		
Cost of car rental		
Industries		

30 Procedures

5.1 Student A: Read this text and complete 7–10 on the flow-chart on page 101.

KEATINGS

> The Project Manager's first task is to choose a contractor to build the store. When this is done, construction work begins. At the same time, the architects plan the layout of the inside of the store. When <u>they</u> have completed the layout, the equipment (e.g. freezers for the store) is ordered. <u>This</u> is done about twenty weeks before the opening date for the store. Then, when the building is ready, <u>it</u> is installed.

5.2 Read the text again. What do the underlined words refer to?

*Example: **they** in line 5 = the architects*

5.3 These sentences are missing from the text. Where do they go?

1 At this stage a schedule of building work is drawn up.

2 A lot of this work is done with computers.

21 Comparing Products and Services

5.3 Student A: Tell your partner about ICS Jetmail's delivery times, weight limit and insurance cover.

Jetmail	

Delivery time
  USA/Europe
  rest of the world
	1–3 days
	up to 10 days

Weight limit?	yes, 20 kg
Insurance cover	up to £250
Do they collect?	5

Sample costs
  5 kg to Germany
  5 kg to Japan
	6
	7

Countries	8

5.4 Now complete the table with the information your partner gives you about Jetmail.

22 Working Practices

7 Student A: Read the report on Greece and complete part C of the table on page 75.

Working around the world – Greece

Working hours
Most people start work at around 8.00 a.m. In the public sector, flexitime is very common so a lot of people start work earlier and can finish between 2.30 and 3.00 p.m. In the private sector, people usually stop work between 3.00 and 5.00 p.m. Not many companies have a lunch hour and most people eat a light snack in their workplace. Because they finish early, many people have a second job which they do in the evening.

Punctuality
Business meetings in Greece do not always start punctually. You should arrive on time for meetings, but be prepared to wait.

Entertaining
Business lunches are not common because few companies have a lunch break. But if you receive an invitation to a restaurant for lunch, remember lunch doesn't usually start until around 2.00 p.m. and it can take all afternoon.

Women in business
There are not many women in top management jobs in Greece.

8.1 Work with a partner. Ask about Ireland and complete part B of the table on page 75.

8.2 Answer your partner's questions about Greece.

Project Unit: A New Office

4.1 Student A: Read this extract from a brochure about office machines and make notes in part A of the table.

The Faxfone 90

The Faxfone 90 is designed for use in small offices or at home. It is available in black or white. It has a 10-number memory for quick and easy dialling. You can fax up to five A4 sheets automatically. It uses a roll of paper. The roll is 210mm wide and 30m long.

With our faxes you can
- avoid postal delays
- communicate quickly and efficiently
- send or receive faxes anywhere in the world

Price	£349.00

	A Faxfone 90	B X50 Fax
For use in		
Choice of colour		
Special features		
Paper roll dimensions		
Price		

4.2 Work with a partner. He/she tells you about the X50 Fax. Make notes in part B of the table.

4.3 Tell your partner about the Faxfone 90.

25 Developments

7.1 Student A: Use this information to answer your partner's questions about Wilcox South-East Asia's performance this year.

Wilcox South-East Asia – Update

Financial overview

A very good year
– turnover up (20%)
– profits up (15%)

Changes and developments in the main markets

Singapore – completed work on a major hotel
Malaysia – won a big contract to build government offices

7.2 Ask your partner questions. Complete the information about Wilcox North America this year.

Wilcox North America – Update

Financial overview

Successful year? Yes/No
Turnover up? Yes/No (.....%)
Profits up? Yes/No (.....%)

Changes and developments in the main markets

USA .....
Canada .....

7.3 Write a fax to Ann Dixon. Explain what has happened in Wilcox North America. Use the information your partner gave you.

Facsimile

Wilcox
International

To: .....
From: .....

Subject: This year's results in Wilcox North America

Financial results
This year .....

Changes and developments in the main markets

30 Procedures

5.1 Student C: Read this text and complete 12–15 on the flow-chart on page 101.

KEATINGS

During the construction stage, the Personnel Department recruits staff for the new store. The new staff are then trained. At the same time, the Publicity Department prepares publicity material for the new store. They advertise it in local newspapers, and on local TV and radio stations. They also plan a special event for the opening of the store. Finally, the new store opens.

5.2 Read the text again. What do the underlined words refer to?

Example: they in line 5 = the Publicity Department

5.3 These sentences are missing from the text. Where do they go?

1 Most of them are recruited locally, but some transfer from other Keatings stores.
2 This is done in Keatings stores in other towns.

115

Tapescripts

1 Jobs and Professions

2.1
Conversation 1

BOB Are you going to Singapore or Jakarta?
ANNE To Jakarta.
BOB Oh, so am I. Are you on holiday?
ANNE No, I'm on business.
BOB Oh, really. What do you do?
ANNE I'm an accountant. I work for Total in Jakarta.

Conversation 2

PAUL Do you work here in Glasgow?
JOHN No, I don't. I work in a hospital in Edinburgh.
PAUL Oh, do you? Do you know Dr Stevens?
JOHN Carl Stevens. Yes, I do. He's my boss.

4.2

HELEN BROWN	I'm Helen Brown. I work for Keatings. I'm a buyer. I buy food products.
MARIE DUVAL	I'm Marie Duval. I work for CFI. I'm an administrator. I organise training courses.
EVA ENGSTROM	I'm Eva Engstrom. I work for PBX. I'm a sales representative. I sell computer systems.
ALEC MACFARLANE	I'm Alec Macfarlane. I work for Wilcox International. I'm an engineer. I manage building projects.
PAT MARCH	I'm Pat March. I work for PBX. I'm an accountant. I do the company accounts.
CHRISTINE SAVILLE	I'm Christine Saville. I work for Park and Moss. I'm a tax expert. I give tax advice.

2 Business Contacts

2.3

ALEC MACFARLANE	About the meeting tomorrow, Tom. Peter Martin... I know the name. Is he a director of Park and Moss?
TOM GRINDLAY	Yes, he is. He works in their London office.
ALEC MACFARLANE	And what about the other people?
TOM GRINDLAY	Well, there's Christine Saville.
ALEC MACFARLANE	What does she do?
TOM GRINDLAY	She's their tax expert, and Karen Page is her assistant.
ALEC MACFARLANE	Right. And where do they work?
TOM GRINDLAY	In the London office with Peter.

ALEC MACFARLANE	I see. What about Wolfgang Binder? Does he work for Park and Moss too?
TOM GRINDLAY	Yes, he does. He's the manager of their office in Germany.
ALEC MACFARLANE	Ah, so he's Klaus Daniel's boss.
TOM GRINDLAY	Yes, that's right.

3
1 She organises training courses.
2 Helen Brown buys food products.
3 Pat March does the company accounts.
4 Christine Saville gives tax advice.
5 He manages building projects.
6 Our secretary types my letters.

6.1

PHILIP ALLEN	So, who's on the course next week?
MARIE DUVAL	Well, there's Anne Leclerc. She's a sales representative for Wilcox International.
PHILIP ALLEN	Sorry, who does she work for?
MARIE DUVAL	Wilcox International. They're in the construction business.
PHILIP ALLEN	Right. And what about Paul Lebrun?
MARIE DUVAL	Paul Lebrun. He's a designer. He works for a company in Lyons.
PHILIP ALLEN	Sorry, what does he do?
MARIE DUVAL	He's a designer. He designs furniture.
PHILIP ALLEN	I see.
MARIE DUVAL	And then there's Marc Roche from Editions Anjou. They're...éditeurs. I don't know the word in English, but they produce books.
PHILIP ALLEN	Ah, a publishing company.
MARIE DUVAL	That's it. I think he's their...

3 Company Information

6.1

MAURIZIO RIVELLA	So, welcome to Reggio Calabria, Mrs Brown.
HELEN BROWN	Thank you. Is this your Head Office?
MAURIZIO RIVELLA	Yes, it is. Our factory is outside the town. We can go there later.
HELEN BROWN	Good. I'd like to visit the factory. How many kilos of pasta does it produce?
MAURIZIO RIVELLA	Three hundred thousand kilos per day.
HELEN BROWN	Oh, a lot! So how many employees do you have?
MAURIZIO RIVELLA	Only seventeen. The factory is very new and we have automated production lines so we don't have many employees.

HELEN BROWN	I see. I know pasta is your main product. Do you have other products?
MAURIZIO RIVELLA	No, we don't. We specialise in pasta.
HELEN BROWN	And where are your main markets?
MAURIZIO RIVELLA	Italy, of course. But we also export to other countries in Europe, the United States and Australia.
HELEN BROWN	That's good.

4 Visits

5.2

PATRICK MULLIGAN	Welcome to Keatings. I'm Patrick Mulligan. How do you do?
PAOLO ROSSO	How do you do, Mr Mulligan?
PATRICK MULLIGAN	The meeting room isn't far from here. Come this way, please. Here we are. Helen Brown will be here soon. Can I take your coat?
PAOLO ROSSO	Oh, thank you.
PATRICK MULLIGAN	Can I get you a coffee?
PAOLO ROSSO	Yes, please.
PATRICK MULLIGAN	Sharon, can you bring us two coffees, please? Ah, here's Helen. Mr Rosso, this is Helen Brown, one of our buyers. Helen, this is Paolo Rosso from Molitano.
HELEN BROWN	Pleased to meet you, Mr Rosso.
PAOLO ROSSO	Pleased to meet you too, Mrs Brown.

5 Routines

5.1

1 I get up at seven.
2 I start work at eight thirty.
3 I have lunch at about one.
4 I leave work at about five o'clock.

6 City Profiles

3.1

Conversation 1

COMMERCIAL ATTACHÉ	Slovak Embassy, Commercial Department. Can I help you?
MARIANNE BOUCHER	Yes. I have a consultancy company here in Brussels. I do research for companies which want to do business in other countries, and I'd like some information about Bratislava.
COMMERCIAL ATTACHÉ	Fine. What would you like to know?
MARIANNE BOUCHER	First, some general questions. What are the main industries around Bratislava?
COMMERCIAL ATTACHÉ	The main ones are engineering,

	chemicals and food processing. And of course agriculture is very important.
MARIANNE BOUCHER	And are there any international companies?
COMMERCIAL ATTACHÉ	Yes, there are about twenty international companies. For example, IBM, Hewlett Packard and Siemens have offices there.
MARIANNE BOUCHER	OK. So now some practical information. What are the working hours of companies?
COMMERCIAL ATTACHÉ	Most offices are open from eight to four thirty. Factories usually open earlier, at seven.
MARIANNE BOUCHER	Fine. Thank you. So now I need to know about…

Conversation 2

MARIANNE BOUCHER	I'm going to Bratislava next week. I know you often go there. Can you give me some help?
DOMINIC WESLEY	Yes, of course. What would you like to know?
MARIANNE BOUCHER	Well, first of all, what's the average cost of a hotel room?
DOMINIC WESLEY	Well, in sterling it's from fifty to a hundred pounds a night.
MARIANNE BOUCHER	Oh, that's quite expensive. And what about getting around the city? Is there an underground?
DOMINIC WESLEY	No, there isn't, but other public transport is good, and taxis aren't expensive.
MARIANNE BOUCHER	OK. I also want to visit some other towns. How much does it cost to rent a car?
DOMINIC WESLEY	For a good car, about forty-five pounds a day.
MARIANNE BOUCHER	Forty-five pounds. OK. And…

6.1

MARIANNE BOUCHER	What about the working hours? When do people start work?
AKIRA NAKATANE	Most Japanese companies are open from nine to five. Some open earlier and some open later, but they don't usually close later than six.
MARIANNE BOUCHER	So the normal hours of business are nine to five?
AKIRA NAKATANE	Yes, that's right.
MARIANNE BOUCHER	I see. Thanks. Now about costs. What's the average cost of a hotel in Tokyo?
AKIRA NAKATANE	I'm not sure, as I don't live in Tokyo. I suppose about fifteen thousand to thirty thousand yen, but I never stay in hotels so I can't be sure about it.

MARIANNE BOUCHER	So that's fifteen thousand for a good hotel?
AKIRA NAKATANE	No, that's not quite right. For a good hotel you pay about thirty thousand yen, I think.
MARIANNE BOUCHER	I see.

8 Entertaining

2.1

JANE	Oh Peter, this is Eva Engstrom. Eva, this is my colleague Peter Simmons.
PETER	How do you do?
EVA	How do you do? What do you think of the conference?
PETER	It's very good. Lots of interesting presentations.
JANE	Can I get you a drink, Eva?
EVA	Yes, please. I'd like a glass of red wine.
JANE	OK. What about you Peter? Would you like another drink?
PETER	No, thanks. I'm fine.
JANE	Excuse me. Could we have two glasses of red wine, please?
BARMAN	Certainly. What kind of red wine would you like?
JANE	Do you have any Spanish wine?
BARMAN	Yes, we have a very good *Rioja*.
JANE	That's fine for me. Do you like Spanish wine, Eva?
EVA	Yes, I do.

4.1

Conversation 1

PETER	What do you do, Eva?
EVA	I'm a sales representative in the Swedish subsidiary.
PETER	Where exactly do you work?
EVA	I work in the Stockholm office.
PETER	I think I know some of the people there. Is Stig Larsson still responsible for sales in Stockholm?
EVA	No, Stig's in Gothenburg now.
PETER	Who's your new boss?
EVA	It's Agnes Miklos.
PETER	I don't know her. Where's she from?
EVA	She's from Hungary.

Conversation 2

PETER	What do you do Eva?
EVA	I'm a sales representative in the Swedish subsidiary.
PETER	In Sweden. Where exactly do you work?
EVA	I work in the Stockholm office.
PETER	Oh, do you? I think I know some of the people there. Is Stig Larsson still responsible for sales in Stockholm?
eva	No, Stig's in Gothenburg now. My new boss is Agnes Miklos. Do you know her?
PETER	Miklos. No, I don't think so. It's an unusual name. Is she Swedish?
EVA	No. Agnes is from Hungary originally, but she lives in Sweden now.

Project Unit: A New Job

5

DAVID MARTIN	OK, Jean-Luc. So you're French and you work in Geneva now. Is that right?
JEAN-LUC PONS	No, that's not quite right. I'm Swiss, but my wife is French and we want to move to France.
DAVID MARTIN	I see. Is French your first language?
JEAN-LUC PONS	Yes, I speak French, German and of course some English.
DAVID MARTIN	OK. And what's your job now?
JEAN-LUC PONS	I work for an international electronics company here in Geneva. I'm a Sales Manager. I'm responsible for sales in Switzerland.
DAVID MARTIN	And what's important for you in a new job?
JEAN-LUC PONS	Well, I want to change industries and I would like a job where I can use my English.
DAVID MARTIN	Yes, your English is very good.
JEAN-LUC PONS	Thank you.
DAVID MARTIN	Anything else?
JEAN-LUC PONS	Well, my wife and I like sports. We often go skiing in the winter. So good holidays are important for us. We also want to live and work in an old place, not a new town.
DAVID MARTIN	I see.

9 Career Development

4

1 He finished his studies last year.
2 He joined the company in May.
3 She started her job last month.
4 He returned to the UK in nineteen ninety-two.
5 I worked in Brazil for six years.
6 They opened another office in France.
7 I transferred to our office in Tokyo.
8 He changed jobs in nineteen eighty-six.

6.2

INTERVIEWER	Can you tell me something about Tim Waterstone?
INTERVIEWEE	Well, he was born in nineteen forty-nine. He studied at Cambridge University. Then, in nineteen sixty-two he decided to go abroad and joined a small company of tea traders in India. I think he stayed in India for four years.
INTERVIEWER	And did he return to the UK after that?
INTERVIEWEE	Yes. He joined Allied Lyons and worked in their Sales Department, but some years later he changed company and moved to WH Smith – the big booksellers.
INTERVIEWER	What was his job there?

INTERVIEWEE	He was responsible for their European division. Then, in nineteen eighty-four he started his own company, Waterstone and Co. He opened bookshops all over Europe. They were very successful.
INTERVIEWER	So when did he decide to sell his company?
INTERVIEWEE	In nineteen eighty-nine. WH Smith agreed to pay twenty-four million pounds for it. It was a very good price in those days.

7.1

DAVID BELLAN	I joined Astral in nineteen seventy-eight.
INTERVIEWER	Was it your first job?
DAVID BELLAN	No, before that I worked for the government.
INTERVIEWER	I see. And were your responsibilities at Astral very different?
DAVID BELLAN	No, not at first. When I joined Astral, I worked in the Accounts Department, but then I transferred to the international trading company. That was very different.
INTERVIEWER	What did you do there?
DAVID BELLAN	I was responsible for crude oil trading in Europe and America.
INTERVIEWER	Did you enjoy the job?
DAVID BELLAN	Yes, I did. It was a very exciting job.
INTERVIEWER	What was your next job?
DAVID BELLAN	Well, in nineteen eighty-five I changed jobs completely and moved to the UK as a distribution manager, but I didn't stay long because the company offered me a very interesting job abroad, in Barbados. I was responsible for all the company's activities in the Caribbean.
INTERVIEWER	That sounds wonderful. How long did you stay?
DAVID BELLAN	Five years. I didn't want to leave, but I returned to the UK last year.

10 Company History

5.1

JOURNALIST	So you took over the family business in nineteen fifty-five?
ENRIQUE BERNAT	No, it was in nineteen fifty-seven. That was when my father retired. The next ten years were very important for Chupa Chups and we built up our business in Spain.
JOURNALIST	So was Spain your only market at that time?
ENRIQUE BERNAT	Yes, we didn't move into foreign markets until the end of the sixties. We built our first factory outside Spain in nineteen...sixty-seven. No, sixty-nine. It was in Bayonne in France.
JOURNALIST	Sorry, I didn't catch that. When did you open the factory?
ENRIQUE BERNAT	In nineteen sixty-nine.
JOURNALIST	Nineteen sixty-nine. I see. Is that the only factory you have outside Spain?
ENRIQUE BERNAT	No, we also have a factory in St Petersburg. We opened there in nineteen ninety-one, but it isn't an easy market and distribution is difficult.
JOURNALIST	I see. What about sales outside Europe?
ENRIQUE BERNAT	Well, Japan is an important market. Our sales were worth twenty million dollars last year. That was a very good result.
JOURNALIST	Sorry, what was the sales figure?
ENRIQUE BERNAT	Twenty million dollars.
JOURNALIST	Twenty million. OK. I've got one final question. Is it true that Salvador Dali designed some of your wrappers?
ENRIQUE BERNAT	Absolutely. It was in the late sixties.

11 Past Performance

3.1

PRESENTER	Car production here was just over eight hundred thousand in nineteen eighty-seven. The following year it went up sharply to over one million cars. This increase did not continue and, for the next three years, output fell steadily to around nine hundred thousand in nineteen ninety-one.
	In nineteen eighty-eight car production rose by nearly a hundred thousand cars. For the next two years production decreased steadily to six hundred and seventy thousand in nineteen ninety. Finally in nineteen ninety-one production went up slightly to seven hundred thousand cars.
	Car manufacturers here built eight hundred thousand cars in nineteen eighty-seven. As you can see, production increased slightly in nineteen eighty-eight, but stayed at the same level in nineteen eighty-nine. For the next two years production levels went up to nearly one point two million in nineteen ninety-one.

12 Small Talk

2.1

TERRY	Hi, Jane. It's nice to see you again. How are you?
JANE	I'm fine. How are you?
TERRY	Fine, thanks. How was the sales conference in Toronto last week?
JANE	It was very interesting, thanks. I spent the weekend there too.
TERRY	Oh, did you? What did you think of Toronto?
JANE	Well, the weather wasn't very good, but it's a very attractive city.

6.1

Conversation 1

KEN   Hi, Jane. How was the sales conference?

JANE   It was very good. I met a lot of interesting people.

KEN   Was Stig Larsson there?

JANE   No, but I met a very nice woman from the Stockholm office who thinks she knows you – Eva Engstrom.

KEN   Eva Engstrom...yes. She joined the company at the same time as me. We were on the same training programme.

Conversation 2

ALEC MACFARLANE   Come in, Christine. How are you?

CHRISTINE SAVILLE   Fine, thanks. It's nice to see you again.

ALEC MACFARLANE   I heard you were on holiday in Crete. It's one of my favourite places. How was the holiday?

CHRISTINE SAVILLE   Excellent. The hotel was very comfortable, the beach was nice and we visited some interesting places.

ALEC MACFARLANE   Did you go to Knossos?

CHRISTINE SAVILLE   Yes, we did. Do you know it?

ALEC MACFARLANE   Yes, it's wonderful. I was there with my family three years ago. What did you think of the food in Crete?

CHRISTINE SAVILLE   Well, I thought it was delicious, but my husband didn't like it.

13 Directions

4.1

1   I work in the Accounts Department. That's on the fourth floor.

2   I work in Reception, on the ground floor.

3   I work on the first floor.

4   I work at the top of the building, on the twenty-second floor.

5   The Sales Department is on the third floor.

6   I work for Max International. Their offices are on the second floor.

7   The company restaurant is on the twentieth floor.

8   My office is on the fourteenth floor.

9   Their offices are on the thirteenth floor.

6.1

VISITOR   Is there a taxi rank near here?

RECEPTIONIST   Yes, there's one just along the road.

VISITOR   Can you tell me how to get there, please?

RECEPTIONIST   Yes, of course. Go out of the building, turn right, and go along boulevard Saint-Michel. There's a taxi rank on the corner of boulevard Saint-Michel and boulevard du Montparnasse.

VISITOR   On the corner of Saint-Michel and Montparnasse.

RECEPTIONIST   Yes, that's right. It's opposite the entrance to the Port Royal RER station.

VISITOR   Fine, thanks for your help.

14 Guidelines

5.1

MR MEYER   Do people speak English at work?

MR SINGH   Oh, yes. Everybody who has an office job can speak some English, and in international companies like yours everybody speaks good English.

MR MEYER   What about dealing with my Indian employees?

MR SINGH   Well, you should always give clear instructions. Avoid asking them to make decisions. In India it's the manager's job to make decisions.

MR MEYER   Ah, very different. I see. And what about colleagues?

MR SINGH   With Indian colleagues you should be friendly. We often meet socially to eat or...

MRS MEYER And are wives invited too?

MR SINGH   Oh, yes. Very often.

MRS MEYER Are there any things that women shouldn't do in India?

MR SINGH   Only a few things...um...you mustn't drink alcohol in public. That makes a very bad impression. And of course you should always wear modest clothes.

MRS MEYER So no short skirts?

MR SINGH   That's right.

MRS MEYER And what about travelling? We'd like to see different parts of India when we're there.

MR SINGH   You should stay in good hotels, and don't forget to take cash. You should always carry cash because not many places take cheques.

15 Telephone Calls

2.1

Conversation 1

CHRISTINE SAVILLE   Tax Department.

WOLFGANG BINDER   Good morning. This is Wolfgang Binder. Is that Christine Saville?

CHRISTINE SAVILLE   Yes, it is. How are you, Wolfgang?

WOLFGANG BINDER   Fine, thanks. How's the weather in England?

CHRISTINE SAVILLE   It's wonderful. Very hot. So, how can I help you, Wolfgang?

WOLFGANG BINDER   Well, I'm calling about your visit next week.

Conversation 2

RECEPTIONIST   Park and Moss, good afternoon.

ALEC MACFARLANE   Good afternoon. I'd like to speak to Christine Saville, please.

RECEPTIONIST   Just a moment, please.

CHRISTINE SAVILLE   Hello, Tax Department.

ALEC MACFARLANE   Hello. This is Alec Macfarlane from Wilcox International.

CHRISTINE SAVILLE   Oh, hello Alec. What can I do for you?

ALEC MACFARLANE   I'd like some information about tax guidelines in Germany.

5.1

Version 1

BA ASSISTANT	British Airways. Reservations. Katerina Manou speaking. How can I help you?
JOE FAIRBANKS	Good morning. My name's Joe Fairbanks. That's F-A-I-R-B-A-N-K-S. I have a flight to London out of Athens on May sixth at ten p.m. It's...um...BA seven five one two. Now I really want to be in London on May sixth, so could you change me to a flight on May fifth? Is that OK?
BA ASSISTANT	Sorry, I didn't catch all of that. Could you speak more slowly, please?

Version 2

BA ASSISTANT	British Airways. Reservations. Katerina Manou speaking. How can I help you?
JOE FAIRBANKS	Hi. I have a ticket for a flight to London and I need to change it. My name's Joe Fairbanks. That's F-A-I-R...
BA ASSISTANT	Sorry. Can I have your flight number first, please?
JOE FAIRBANKS	Oh, yes. It's BA seven five one two to London.
BA ASSISTANT	BA seven five one two. OK. And the date?
JOE FAIRBANKS	Well, I have a booking for May sixth, but I really want to be in London on May sixth, so I want to fly the day before.
BA ASSISTANT	Sorry. Could you repeat the dates, please?
JOE FAIRBANKS	I want to change my flight from May sixth to May fifth.
BA ASSISTANT	I see. OK. Can I have your name again, please?
JOE FAIRBANKS	Yes. It's Joe Fairbanks.
BA ASSISTANT	Could you spell that, please?
JOE FAIRBANKS	F-A-I-R-B-A-N-K-S.
BA ASSISTANT	That's fine, Mr Fairbanks. Hold on, please. I'll check availability for that.

6.3

B C D E G P T V
F L M N S X Z
A J K H
Q U W
The letters left are I Y O R.

16 Offers and Requests

4.1

1 I'll give you my number. It's two-oh-three seven-six-five-seven-five-nine.
2 Sorry, did you say three-oh-one nine-seven-six-seven-double five?
3 My phone number is three-oh-two seven-six-double-five-seven-nine.
4 Could you call me on three-oh-two seven-five-seven-five-nine-five?

5.2

RICHARD CARTER	I'd like to speak to Andy Mitchell. Is he in the office?
RECEPTIONIST	No, I'm sorry he's not here today.
RICHARD CARTER	Oh, dear. This is Richard Carter. I need to speak to him.
RECEPTIONIST	Would you like his home number, Mr Carter?
RICHARD CARTER	No, it's OK thank you. Could you tell him I called and ask him to ring me tomorrow morning? The number is oh-nine-one five-six-eight-double four.
RECEPTIONIST	Yes, of course Mr Carter. I'll give him the message.

Project Unit: A Top Firm

4

INGMAR BORG	So what would you like to know about Ikea?
INTERVIEWER	Well, first of all, something about the history.
INGMAR BORG	Yes. As you probably know, Ingvar Kamprad started the company in nineteen forty-three, but it was very different then. The first furniture store opened in nineteen fifty-three in a town in the south of Sweden. This was successful, so he opened another, very big store outside Stockholm in nineteen sixty-five. Soon after that Ikea opened stores in other parts of Sweden and also in Norway and Denmark.
INTERVIEWER	I see. And when did Ikea open its first store outside Scandinavia?
INGMAR BORG	In nineteen seventy-three in Switzerland. That was the first of many.
INTERVIEWER	OK. What about factories? When did you open your first factory abroad?
INGMAR BORG	Oh, we don't have any factories. We don't manufacture the furniture ourselves. We buy components from suppliers and assemble them.
INTERVIEWER	Oh, that's interesting. So you only have stores. How many do you have now?
INGMAR BORG	A hundred and eleven stores in twenty-four different countries. We make nearly eighty per cent of our sales in Europe, but we also have stores in other places, such as Canada, the United States and Kuwait.
INTERVIEWER	And is it still a family firm?
INGMAR BORG	Oh, yes. It's very important to Mr Kamprad to keep the family business atmosphere. In fact, his three sons all work for Ikea.

17 Plans

2.2

JONATHAN FOX	What do you think about the outline programme for the quality control seminar?
PATRICK MULLIGAN	It looks fine, but I've got a few questions.
JONATHAN FOX	Yes.
PATRICK MULLIGAN	What are the delegates doing on Sunday evening?
HELEN BROWN	There's no special programme because the coach isn't arriving at the hotel until about nine thirty p.m.
PATRICK MULLIGAN	OK, I see. And, who's giving the opening speech? Is it me?
JONATHAN FOX	No, it's the Managing Director. You're giving the presentation on quality control at the end of the morning.
PATRICK MULLIGAN	Fine. Now, where are we having the reception?
JONATHAN FOX	At Kilkenny Castle. We booked it last week. We're also planning to invite the mayor of Kilkenny but we're not sure if he can come.
PATRICK MULLIGAN	That sounds good. Which supplier are you planning to visit?
HELEN BROWN	Probably McCormack's. I'm seeing John McCormack tomorrow to discuss it.
PATRICK MULLIGAN	Right. So are they having lunch in the hotel on Tuesday?
HELEN BROWN	We're not sure. It depends on the morning programme.
PATRICK MULLIGAN	OK. That sounds fine. By the way, Helen, is my old friend Maurizio Rivella coming?
HELEN BROWN	Yes, he is. But he isn't arriving until Tuesday morning.

3

1 He's returning to London this Tuesday.
2 She's starting a new job on Friday.
3 Tom's staying at the Central Hotel.
4 Who's going to the meeting next Monday?
5 They're leaving the hotel after lunch.
6 What are you doing on Thursday?
7 What time are you leaving work today?
8 I'm meeting David at the station.
9 Am I giving a presentation at the meeting?

18 Appointments

2.2

LANA RUSSELL	Is that Charles Cameron?
CHARLES CAMERON	Yes, it is.
LANA RUSSELL	Hello, this is Lana Russell from Interconsult.
CHARLES CAMERON	Oh, hello, Lana. What can I do for you?
LANA RUSSELL	It's about the Japanese company I talked to you about last week.
CHARLES CAMERON	Yes. I remember.
LANA RUSSELL	Well, two of the management team are coming here in early September and they'd like to meet you.
CHARLES CAMERON	Oh, that's good news. When are they coming?
LANA RUSSELL	They're planning to be here from Tuesday the seventh to Thursday the ninth.
CHARLES CAMERON	The seventh to the ninth of September. I'll get my diary. Oh, Tuesday's not possible. I'm visiting clients in Birmingham all day.
LANA RUSSELL	OK. What about Wednesday?
CHARLES CAMERON	Wednesday's OK, but the morning's a bit difficult.
LANA RUSSELL	How about the afternoon then?
CHARLES CAMERON	Yes, that's OK.
LANA RUSSELL	What time?
CHARLES CAMERON	Let me see. Is two thirty OK?
LANA RUSSELL	Yes, I think that's fine. I'll send a fax to Japan and call you later in the week to confirm.

5.1

IAN CAMPBELL	When are they coming?
LANA RUSSELL	From Tuesday the seventh to Thursday the ninth.
IAN CAMPBELL	Just a minute. I'll get my diary. Right. Let me see. Well, Tuesday's no good. I'm at a seminar until Wednesday lunchtime.
LANA RUSSELL	Are you coming back to the office in the afternoon?
IAN CAMPBELL	No, the seminar is in London and I'm driving back to Glasgow.
LANA RUSSELL	OK. How about Thursday then?
IAN CAMPBELL	Yes, that's fine, but I prefer the morning.
LANA RUSSELL	OK. Is ten o'clock OK?
IAN CAMPBELL	Hm. Actually it's a bit early. Can we say eleven o'clock?
LANA RUSSELL	OK. I'll send a fax to Japan and call you again to confirm.

5.4

IAN CAMPBELL	When are they coming?
LANA RUSSELL	From Tuesday the seventh to Thursday the ninth.

IAN CAMPBELL Just a minute. I'll get my diary. Right. Let me see. Well, Tuesday's no good. I'm at a seminar until Wednesday lunchtime.

LANA RUSSELL Are you coming back to the office in the afternoon?

IAN CAMPBELL No, the seminar is in London and I'm driving back to Glasgow.

LANA RUSSELL OK. So Tuesday and Wednesday aren't possible. How about Thursday then?

IAN CAMPBELL Yes, that's fine, but I prefer the morning.

LANA RUSSELL OK. So Thursday morning. Is ten o'clock OK?

IAN CAMPBELL Hm. Actually it's a bit early. Can we say eleven o'clock?

LANA RUSSELL Eleven o'clock. OK. So that's eleven o'clock on Thursday the ninth. I'll send a fax to Japan and call you again to confirm.

19 Products

4.1

CUSTOMER I like the machine, but I'm not sure I have enough space for it. What's the height of it?

SALESMAN It's seven hundred and forty millimetres high.

CUSTOMER Seven hundred and forty millimetres. That's OK. And what's the depth of it?

SALESMAN Five hundred and five millimetres.

CUSTOMER Aha. And how wide is it?

SALESMAN The width is four hundred and thirty-five millimetres.

6

RENZO FABBRI Café Express. Renzo Fabbri speaking.

BOB TEMPLE Good morning. My name's Bob Temple and I'm calling from Seattle. I saw your advertisement in *Catering News* and I'm interested in your coffee machines.

RENZO FABBRI Oh, yes. Well, we have a wide range of different machines, so if you can tell me a little about your business, I can make some suggestions.

BOB TEMPLE Sure. I have a coffee bar here in Seattle and I'm planning to open two more later in the year.

RENZO FABBRI Hm. What kind of coffee do you sell at the moment?

BOB TEMPLE Mainly filter, but I want to get into espresso. That's really popular now up here.

RENZO FABBRI OK, so you want a machine for making espresso.

BOB TEMPLE Yeah. Not only espresso. Lots of people here like milk in their coffee, so I really need a machine which can make cappuccino too.

RENZO FABBRI OK. No problem. And how many cups do you need to be able to make?

BOB TEMPLE It depends on the time of day. We're open from ten to seven and we're busy first thing when we open, again around lunchtime, and when people leave work. So at those times about a hundred cups an hour, I guess. Not so many at other times of the day.

RENZO FABBRI And do you have waiters serving the coffee or do customers help themselves?

BOB TEMPLE No, it's all waiter service.

RENZO FABBRI So at busy times, it's important for you to be able to prepare coffee quickly?

BOB TEMPLE Yeah, that's right, but the coffee's got to taste good too. That's really important.

RENZO FABBRI OK, I think I have just the machine for you. It's the...

20 Invitations

2.1

Conversation 1

BOB TEMPLE Good. I think that's everything we need to discuss now. By the way, Renzo, would you like to have dinner at my house tomorrow?

RENZO FABBRI Thank you, but I'm flying back to San Francisco this evening.

BOB TEMPLE Oh, that's a pity. Maybe on your next visit, then.

Conversation 2

CHRISTINE SAVILLE OK, Wolfgang, let's call it a day. Would you like to go out for a meal later on? Perhaps Peter can come too.

WOLFGANG BINDER Thank you. That's a good idea.

Conversation 3

LANA RUSSELL Ian, I'm calling about the visit of Mr Noguchi and Mr Miyazawa. It's confirmed for Wednesday the eighth of September at two thirty.

IAN CAMPBELL Excellent. Thank you very much. By the way, I'd like to discuss some points about their visit with you. Would you like to meet for lunch one day next week?

LANA RUSSELL That would be very nice.

4.2

SUE I like classical music.

TIM What about jazz?

SUE I'm not very keen on jazz.

TIM Do you like Italian films?

SUE Yes! I really like Italian films.

TIM What about opera?

SUE I don't like opera very much.

5.2

IRENA SUSKOVA Emma, I know you're staying here in Bratislava for the weekend. Do you have any plans for Saturday?

EMMA JONES Well, I'm planning to do some sightseeing, of course. I'm not sure after that.

IRENA SUSKOVA	Would you like to go out together on Saturday night?
EMMA JONES	Thank you. That's a good idea.
IRENA SUSKOVA	OK. Do you like opera?

5.5

Version 1

IRENA SUSKOVA	OK. Do you like opera?
EMMA JONES	Yes, I really like opera.
IRENA SUSKOVA	Oh, good. Well, *Tosca* is on at the opera house here. Would you like to go to that if I can get tickets?
EMMA JONES	That would be very nice.

Version 2

IRENA SUSKOVA	OK. Do you like opera?
EMMA JONES	No, I'm not very keen on opera.
IRENA SUSKOVA	Would you like to go out for dinner then?
EMMA JONES	That would be very nice.

21 Comparing Products and Services

3.1

JANET PARKER	We use Worldpost at the moment, but we sometimes need a faster service.
ASSISTANT	OK. Well, you could try Superpost. The delivery is quicker than Worldpost. Parcels take a day to the USA or Europe, and two days to the rest of the world.
JANET PARKER	That's good. And can you send parcels heavier than thirty kilograms?
ASSISTANT	Yes, you can. There's no weight limit.
JANET PARKER	OK. What about insurance cover? Some of the things we send are very expensive.
ASSISTANT	The insurance cover is better than Worldpost: up to five thousand pounds per parcel.
JANET PARKER	Excellent. And do you collect?
ASSISTANT	Yes. Just call us and we'll come to your office.
JANET PARKER	Good. That's more convenient than going to your office. Now, what about the cost?
ASSISTANT	Well, of course Superpost is more expensive than Worldpost.
JANET PARKER	Can you give me some examples? How much is it for, say, a five kilogram parcel to Germany or Japan?
ASSISTANT	Hold on, please. Right. To Germany thirty-nine pounds eighty and to Japan eighty-eight pounds forty.
JANET PARKER	Germany thirty-nine pounds eighty and Japan eighty-eight pounds forty. Yes, that *is* expensive!
ASSISTANT	Yes, but Superpost takes less time.
JANET PARKER	True. OK. One more thing. We have to send things to a lot of different countries all over the world. Does Superpost cover the same countries as Worldpost?
ASSISTANT	No. In fact, Worldpost covers more countries. Superpost is available for a hundred and sixty countries. I'll send you a list of them if you like.
JANET PARKER	Thanks. That would be helpful.

22 Working Practices

6

JULIA	So do people start work early in the Netherlands?
FRANK	Earlier than here in the UK. Officially, the working hours are eight thirty to five, but in fact many managers start earlier, at around eight.
JULIA	I see. So does that mean people aren't in their offices late?
FRANK	That's right. Working late isn't usual. It isn't part of the culture. Of course, if there's something important to do, people stay later.
JULIA	What about holidays?
FRANK	They get more holiday than us. Most Dutch managers take five or six weeks holiday a year. The most popular time is from the middle of July to the end of August, so that's a really slow time for business.
JULIA	Oh, I'm surprised. I thought a long summer break was more typical for southern European countries. What about meetings and appointments? Are people generally punctual?
FRANK	Yes. The Dutch are always on time, so you should be too. Punctuality is something that's considered very important.
JULIA	Fine. I'll remember that. Do Dutch people do a lot of business entertaining?
FRANK	Some, but business lunches aren't common. In fact, if you are at a meeting, you often work through lunch. People don't like to stop for lunch, and often just have a sandwich at their desks. Most business entertainment is after work – people prefer to go out for dinner in the evening, after the business is finished.
JULIA	That's useful to know. I've got one last question. Are there many women managers in the Netherlands?
FRANK	No, surprisingly not, but there are some women with good jobs in law and the media.

23 Discussions

3.1

CHRIS TAYLOR	Right, we have three main suggestions to discuss. The first is a crèche. The second is career breaks. And finally, teleworking. OK. Can you start, Pat? What do you think about setting up a crèche in the company?

PAT MARCH A crèche is an excellent idea. I know a lot of women leave the company when they have children because it's so difficult to find somebody to look after their children.

JOHN BEATTY Yes, I agree with Pat. It's a problem for women in my department too.

CHRIS TAYLOR So you think that a crèche is one solution. Of course, we need to look at the costs. OK. What about career breaks?

PAT MARCH Well, I like the idea. I know some companies, like Wilcox International for example, have successful career break programmes. Women, and men, can have up to five years away from their jobs. So I think it's a possible solution.

JOHN BEATTY I don't really agree. Companies like Wilcox International are not in the computer business. Computer technology changes very quickly, so long periods away from work are not practical. So I don't think career breaks are a good idea for us.

PAT MARCH Yes, you're right. I didn't think of that.

CHRIS TAYLOR I agree. So it seems that career breaks are not practical for PBX. We'll drop that suggestion. What do you think about teleworking then?

JOHN BEATTY I think it's a good solution. My programmers can easily work from home.

PAT MARCH I agree. We can do a lot of the accounts from home too.

CHRIS TAYLOR That's true, but staff from some departments can't work from home. In Personnel, for example, I need to meet the staff. So you like the idea, but I think we need to talk to more departments.

7.1

Discussion 1

ALAN What do you think about setting up a crèche in the company, Brenda?

BRENDA I don't think it's a good idea. Most of the women in my department have older children who are at school.

CHARLES Yes, you're right. And setting up a crèche is very expensive.

Discussion 2

ALAN What do you think about introducing flexitime, Brenda?

BRENDA I like the idea. In the sales team we can easily start and finish work at different times.

CHARLES I agree with Brenda. Flexitime is a possible solution in my department too.

Discussion 3

CHARLES What do you think about asking an external catering company to run our canteen? I know Keatings did that and their canteen is very successful now.

BRENDA I like the idea. It's a good way to cut the company's costs and have better food too.

ALAN That's true, but employees often pay more for their food. I think we need to get more information about food prices.

7.3

Discussion 1

CHARLES Yes, you're right. And setting up a crèche is very expensive.

ALAN So you don't think this is a good idea for us.

Discussion 2

CHARLES I agree with Brenda. Flexitime is a possible solution in my department too.

ALAN So we agree that flexitime is a good idea.

Discussion 3

ALAN That's true, but the employees often pay more for their food. I think we need to get more information about food prices.

CHARLES So you like the idea, Brenda, but Alan thinks we need more information about food prices.

24 Restaurants

3.1

PATRICK MULLIGAN So, what would you like as a starter, Maurizio?

MAURIZIO RIVELLA Let me see. What do you recommend, Patrick?

PATRICK MULLIGAN Well, you could try the grilled prawns. They're very good here.

MAURIZIO RIVELLA I'm not very keen on seafood.

PATRICK MULLIGAN Well, why don't you try the leek and potato soup then? It's home-made and a speciality of this restaurant.

MAURIZIO RIVELLA That sounds good. I'll try that.

PATRICK MULLIGAN OK. And for your main course. What would you like?

MAURIZIO RIVELLA I think I'll have the steak.

PATRICK MULLIGAN OK. And would you like vegetables with it?

MAURIZIO RIVELLA No, I'll just have a salad.

6.1

Conversation 1

GUEST What's *gado-gado*?

HOST That's an Indonesian dish. It's a salad of cooked, green vegetables and...eggs. I don't know the word in English, but it's when you boil the eggs in water for a long time.

GUEST Ah, you mean hard-boiled eggs.

HOST Yes, hard-boiled eggs. And it's served cold with a special peanut sauce.

GUEST That sounds very unusual.

HOST Unusual, but delicious.

Conversation 2

GUEST What's typically Swedish on this menu?

125

HOST Well, what about *Jansson's Frestelse?* That's Jansson's temptation in English.

GUEST Jansson's temptation! That sounds interesting. What is it?

HOST Well, we eat it as a main course. It's made with potatoes, onions, anchovies and cream. It's baked in the oven. It's a simple dish, but it tastes very good.

Conversation 3

GUEST What's shrimp cocktail?

HOST Right. Do you know what prawns are?

GUEST Yes.

HOST OK. Well, shrimps are similar to prawns, but they're smaller. And shrimp cocktail is cold, cooked shrimps in a pink sauce similar to mayonnaise. It's served with some lettuce.

LEARNING TIP

WAITRESS Would you like anything else, sir?

GUEST Yes, I'd like a desert, please.

WAITER What?!

Project Unit: A New Office

1

ALISON KEILER Is that Ian Brown?

IAN BROWN Yes, it is.

ALISON KEILER Hello, Ian. This is Alison Keiler from Ace Advertising.

IAN BROWN Oh, hello, Alison. How are you?

ALISON KEILER Very well, thanks. And you?

IAN BROWN Fine, thanks. Very busy.

ALISON KEILER Not too busy, I hope, because I'm calling about our new office.

IAN BROWN Yes?

ALISON KEILER Well, we're planning to buy an old warehouse outside the town. At the moment it's basically four walls and a roof. We'd like to convert it into a new office. Could you do the design for us?

IAN BROWN Yes, of course. That sounds very interesting.

ALISON KEILER Good. So can we meet?

IAN BROWN Certainly. Just a moment, I'll get my diary. Right. How about the week after next?

ALISON KEILER Yes. Let me see. Tuesday's the best day for me.

IAN BROWN So Tuesday the fifteenth.

ALISON KEILER No, that's next week. The week after it's the twenty-second.

IAN BROWN Of course! Sorry. Yes, that's fine. How about ten o'clock?

ALISON KEILER Ten o'clock. No, that's not possible. I'm having a meeting with a client in the morning. I know, would you like to meet for lunch, then we can talk after lunch?

IAN BROWN That would be very nice. Where do you want to meet?

ALISON KEILER I'll pick you up at your office at about twelve thirty.

IAN BROWN So that's twelve thirty on Tuesday the twenty-second at my office.

ALISON KEILER That's right.

25 Developments

5.1

ANN DIXON This is Ann Dixon, from publicity. I'm collecting information for the next edition of the company magazine. I'd like some information about Wilcox Far East.

JACK NOLAN Sure. What would you like to know?

ANN DIXON Well, has it been a successful year for you?

JACK NOLAN Yes, in general it has. We've expanded our business and won several new contracts in new markets.

ANN DIXON Good. So has your turnover gone up?

JACK NOLAN Yes, it has. In fact, it's increased by five per cent.

ANN DIXON Have your profits gone up too?

JACK NOLAN No, they haven't, but they've stayed at the same level.

ANN DIXON I see. And what's happened in Japan?

JACK NOLAN Well, the Japanese market hasn't been good for us this year. There's a lot of competition in the construction business. But we've done well in Hong Kong. We've won an exciting contract to build a big hotel and shopping centre.

26 Progress Reports

3.1

Conversation 1

STANLEY TAM Hello. This is Stanley Tam.

MARIANNE BOUCHER Hello, Mr Tam. What can I do for you?

STANLEY TAM Well, I'm calling about the recruitment. Have you received the text for the advertisement?

MARIANNE BOUCHER Yes, I have. It arrived two days ago and I've already placed the advertisement in the newspaper.

STANLEY TAM Good. That's all I wanted to know for the moment. Thanks for your help. I'll call you at the beginning of next week to check progress.

Conversation 2

STANLEY TAM So what's happened on the recruitment?

MARIANNE BOUCHER It's going very well. We've received a lot of applications and I've already spoken to the good candidates on the phone.

STANLEY TAM	Excellent. Have you prepared a short-list yet?
MARIANNE BOUCHER	No, I haven't done that yet. I'm waiting for more applications.
STANLEY TAM	What about the interviews? Have you decided where to hold them?
MARIANNE BOUCHER	Yes, I've already booked a meeting room at the Grand Hotel on Friday the twenty-sixth of April. What about your flight to Belgium?
STANLEY TAM	I haven't booked it yet, but now I have the date for the interviews I'll get my secretary to do it.

5

MARIANNE BOUCHER	How's progress on the recruitment for Mr Tam?
DAVID SKINNER	Fine. I've phoned all the candidates on the short-list.
MARIANNE BOUCHER	Good. And have you typed a schedule for the interviews?
DAVID SKINNER	I haven't had time to do that yet, but I'll do it this afternoon.
MARIANNE BOUCHER	Fine. Have you written to the unsuccessful candidates?
DAVID SKINNER	No, not yet. There are a lot of them.
MARIANNE BOUCHER	Don't worry. It's not very urgent. You can do it next week. OK. Now, what about the arrangements for the interviews? Have you booked a room for Mr Tam at the Grand?
DAVID SKINNER	No, he hasn't given me his flight times yet.
MARIANNE BOUCHER	I see. Why don't you phone him again?
DAVID SKINNER	OK. I'll do that this afternoon.
MARIANNE BOUCHER	And one more thing, the refreshments. Have you ordered coffee at the hotel?
DAVID SKINNER	Yes, I've done that.
MARIANNE BOUCHER	And lunch. Is that booked?

27 Business Analysis

2.2

Graph 1

PRESENTER	We launched this product the year before last. Last year sales remained constant because the product was not well known. This year sales have risen because of our advertisements on TV.

Graph 2

PRESENTER	We launched this product three years ago. Last year sales rose because of a price reduction. But this year sales have remained constant because competition has increased.

28 Out and About

4.1

WOLFGANG BINDER	Are you enjoying living in Germany?
ALEC MACFARLANE	Yes, very much.
WOLFGANG BINDER	Have you had time to look round the city?
ALEC MACFARLANE	Yes, a little.
WOLFGANG BINDER	What have you seen?
ALEC MACFARLANE	My wife and I went to the modern art gallery on Saturday.
WOLFGANG BINDER	So you like art?
ALEC MACFARLANE	Yes, we do.
WOLFGANG BINDER	Have you also been to Museum Ludwig?
ALEC MACFARLANE	No.
WOLFGANG BINDER	Well, I think you should go there some time.

4.3

WOLFGANG BINDER	Are you enjoying living in Germany?
ALEC MACFARLANE	Yes, very much, but we've been very busy.
WOLFGANG BINDER	Have you had time to look round the city?
ALEC MACFARLANE	Yes, a little. My wife and I really like art so we went to the modern art gallery on Saturday. It has an interesting collection.
WOLFGANG BINDER	Yes, I like it too. Have you also been to Museum Ludwig?
ALEC MACFARLANE	Museum Ludwig. No. Where's that?
WOLFGANG BINDER	It's in Cologne. I think it's the best modern art gallery in Germany. You should go there some time. It's not far by train.

30 Procedures

2.1

INTERVIEWER	What new projects are you working on?
BUYER	We're developing a new range of clothes for the autumn.
INTERVIEWER	That sounds interesting. What does that involve?
BUYER	Well let's take a woollen jacket as an example. In the spring, the design team visits fashion shows. They choose the new style and colours and produce a design brief. After that a wool supplier is chosen.
INTERVIEWER	And where do you come in?
BUYER	At the next stage. I choose the manufacturer. We talk together and draw up a production schedule. Next the contract is signed and production begins.
INTERVIEWER	So how many jackets are produced?
BUYER	Normally about twenty thousand, in two or three colours.

INTERVIEWER	What happens next?
BUYER	When they're ready, the jackets are delivered to our warehouse, and then they're distributed to our stores in Ireland and abroad.

31 Solutions

2.1

ANNE	Thank you for your presentation, Dagmar. I think we all have a clear idea now of the traffic problems here in Paxford. Bill and Carlo – you studied other towns' solutions to traffic problems. So now I'd like to hear your suggestions.
BILL	Well, I think people in cars should pay a toll to enter the business and shopping areas. They do that in Oslo.
CARLO	That's right. Singapore has that system too. And I've got another suggestion. Some towns, like Florence for example, have banned all traffic from central areas during the daytime. I think we should do that here too – ban all traffic from the historic centre.
ANNE	So, we've got two suggestions so far. One is to ban all cars completely from the historic centre in the daytime. The other is to control traffic in the business and shopping areas by making cars pay a toll to enter. Any other ideas?
CARLO	We could make parking in the centre more expensive.
DAGMAR	I don't really agree. All these ideas will be very unpopular with drivers.
ANNE	Hold on, Dagmar. Can we keep the discussion for later? I just want ideas at the moment, then we'll discuss all of them. Bill, you had another suggestion.
BILL	Yes. We could build more car parks outside the town.
ANNE	OK. Anything else?

4.1

ANNE	OK. We've got six suggestions now. Let's discuss them in more detail. What do you think about the first suggestion – making cars pay a toll to enter the business and shopping areas?
DAGMAR	I'm worried about people who live in these areas. I don't think it's fair for them to pay a toll for their cars. I think we should...
ANNE	Yes?
DAGMAR	Hm...
CARLO	I agree with Dagmar. It's not fair. I think we should give the people a...let me think...a...oh, what do you call it?...a special permission to enter the area for people who live there.
BILL	A resident's permit?
CARLO	That's it. A resident's permit.
DAGMAR	Yes. That's what I wanted to say, too.

32 Closing Stages

2.1

MARIANNE BOUCHER	I thought the interviews went very well.
STANLEY TAM	Yes, the candidates were all very good. I was very pleased.
MARIANNE BOUCHER	Good. So, before you leave I'd like to summarise a few points.
STANLEY TAM	OK.
MARIANNE BOUCHER	So, we've agreed that you'll call me on Friday with the names of the successful candidates.
STANLEY TAM	Yes. I'll speak to Mr Shee as soon as I get back and we'll make a decision.
MARIANNE BOUCHER	OK. And then I'll phone the successful candidates and offer them the jobs.
STANLEY TAM	Fine.
MARIANNE BOUCHER	OK. I think that's all for now.
STANLEY TAM	Fine. So thanks for all your help with the arrangements, Mrs Boucher.
MARIANNE BOUCHER	That's OK, Mr Tam. I'm glad we could help.
STANLEY TAM	Goodbye, Mrs Boucher. I'll speak to you again on Friday.
MARIANNE BOUCHER	Goodbye, Mr Tam. Have a good flight back to Hong Kong.
STANLEY TAM	Thanks.

4.2

1 He'll send you a copy of the report.
2 You'll meet him tomorrow.
3 They'll contact you on Monday.
4 We'll arrange a meeting for next week.
5 She'll call you this afternoon.
6 I'll speak to him after lunch.

Project Unit: A Product Launch

4

PRODUCTION MANAGER	I'd like to explain the procedure for packaging and distributing AQUA-C, our latest range of fruit-flavoured bottled water.

The bottles are delivered to our plant near Matlock from a supplier in Northampton. The labels are sent to us from a printing company in Holland. As you know, the water is bottled, packed and then labelled in the plant. After that, the bottled water for the UK market is stored in our warehouse at the plant, for distribution to supermarkets and breweries, and for our own local door-to-door service. The rest of the bottled water goes to our other warehouse in Harwich. From there it is shipped to our customers' warehouses in Holland, Germany and the Middle East. They organise the final distribution of AQUA-C to shops and supermarkets there.